FAITH AND WRESTLING

HOW THE ROLE OF A WRESTLER MIRRORS THE CHRISTIAN LIFE

MICHAEL FESSLER

WESTBOW
PRESS®
A DIVISION OF THOMAS NELSON
& ZONDERVAN

Scriptures taken from the Holy Bible, New International Version®, NIV®. Copyright © 1973, 1978, 1984, 2011 by Biblica, Inc.™ Used by permission of Zondervan. All rights reserved worldwide. www.zondervan.com The "NIV" and "New International Version" are trademarks registered in the United States Patent and Trademark Office by Biblica, Inc.™ All rights reserved.

WestBow Press books may be ordered through booksellers or by contacting:

WestBow Press
A Division of Thomas Nelson & Zondervan
1663 Liberty Drive
Bloomington, IN 47403
www.westbowpress.com
1 (866) 928-1240

Because of the dynamic nature of the Internet, any web addresses or links contained in this book may have changed since publication and may no longer be valid. The views expressed in this work are solely those of the author and do not necessarily reflect the views of the publisher, and the publisher hereby disclaims any responsibility for them.

Any people depicted in stock imagery provided by Thinkstock are models, and such images are being used for illustrative purposes only. Certain stock imagery © Thinkstock.

ISBN: 978-1-4908-9621-2 (sc)
ISBN: 978-1-4908-9620-5 (e)

Print information available on the last page.

WestBow Press rev. date: 09/23/2015

CONTENTS

The Christian Wrestler Life Verse

And he died for all, *that those who live should no longer live for themselves but for him who died for them and was raised again* ... Therefore, if anyone is in Christ, *the new creation has come*: The old has gone, the new is here! All this is from God, who reconciled us to himself through Christ and gave us the ministry of reconciliation: that God was reconciling the world to himself in Christ, not counting people's sins against them. And he has committed to us the message of reconciliation. *We are therefore Christ's ambassadors,* as though God were making his appeal through us. We implore you on Christ's behalf: *Be reconciled to God.*

—2 Corinthians 5:15, 17–20, emphasis mine

ACKNOWLEDGMENTS

First of all, I would like to thank God. This book started out as merely an inspirational idea about four years ago. No matter what happens, it is my fervent belief that God put the passion for this project on my heart, and He never allowed this passion to falter. It was a slow process, one filled with plenty of uncertainty. However, the writing and completion of this work is one step in the direction of obedience to my Creator. The next step is to get this book into the hands of others who will benefit from its content. Therefore, those who have taken the time to read this book, thank you! You are helping me remain faithful to the call that God has placed on my heart.

I would also like to thank Jack Spates. Without his encouragement and belief in this book, I am almost certain it would never have reached publication. He has become a dear friend of mine. Jack's story is also highlighted within these pages, and I am thankful that he allowed me to include his experience. And that goes for the others who graciously allowed me to tell their stories. Nate and Jayson, thank you so much!

Thank you to Athletes in Action (AIA), especially Rob Bronson and Gene Davis for your willingness to support this project and endeavor. I am incredibly grateful!

Thank you to the love of my life, Kristin. You believe that I have something to say, something that could potentially change the lives of others. I love and appreciate you!

Thank you to all my friends and family. A loving community is necessary for any person, and I have that. I love you!

INTRODUCTION

F aith and wrestling—what's the relationship between the two? Rather than an inquiry that has people aspiring for answers regarding the relevance or functionality of this relationship, the connection between faith and wrestling becomes increasingly evident as one looks for it. Faith and wrestling have the tendency to contain somewhat of a mutual interplay, in that wrestling appears to be a physical mirroring of what so many of us combat with spiritually. And a great number of wrestlers have found it pertinent to express their faith alongside their competitive arena.

Faith is something that we live out through a certain set of beliefs. If truly a part of one's life, it should have a propensity to direct one's decisions, both big and small, and deeply influence how one approaches life. Wrestling, on the other hand, is a sport. Yet anyone who has experienced it knows it's so much more than that. It directly impacts other areas of one's life, whether related to diet, social life, sleep regimen, etc. Furthermore, it's a character builder. There's the saying "Anybody can beat anybody on any given day," and given the talent and devotion of wrestlers, I find this to be true today more than ever. Sure, there are those who have managed to break away from the pack and have found winning matches to be a matter of expectation. However, even legends fall. And we know this to be true because we've seen it. From Dan Gable to Cael Sanderson, Buvaisar Saitiev to Alexander Karelin, every legend of wrestling has experienced the heavy weight of defeat. And it's how they have dealt with that defeat that speaks of their level of character.

To say that wrestling is a character builder is not to suggest that all wrestlers are altogether good people. One would be hard-pressed to hold such a position. However, at the very least, given the unique individualistic quality of the sport, one could say that wrestling allows the opportunity for people to *develop* their character in a very real and practical way, and whether they respond in a manner that is appropriate, or even good, is up to them.

There's something extremely inimitable about wrestling. And while its popularity may never reach the heights of, say, football or baseball, it most certainly will forever have a special place in the world of sports. There's too much that it offers that other sports don't seem to have the ability to, at least not to the same extent. It's all-consuming. It demands every facet of one's competitive nature: mind, body, and soul. Furthermore, to be a wrestler is to assume the title as a significant aspect of one's identity. Whether you are still competing or not, it becomes a part of what makes you who you are. In other words, *wrestler* is attached to your identity.

In the same way, faith can be described in a similar light, only to a more significant level. For while the relationship between faith and wrestling is a thriving one, faith must take the leading role.

As previously suggested, I am not speaking of a flimsy faith. I am not talking about faith as a category in one's interests or a simple belief in a supreme being. I'm talking about something that has driving force. I'm talking about an all-consuming faith, one that interferes with our desire to be the masters of our own lives, one that causes us to live a certain way, one that allows God to change who we are. I'm talking about a faith that demands sacrifice, that demands a fervent devotion to becoming a person more resembling of Christ. The late Christian author Brennan Manning once wrote,

> If a random sampling of one thousand American Christians were taken today, the majority would define faith as belief in the existence of God. In earlier times it did not take faith to believe that God existed—almost everybody took that for granted. Rather, faith had to do with one's relationship to God—whether one trusted in God. The difference between faith as 'belief in something that may or may not exist' and faith as 'trusting in God' is enormous. The first is a matter of the head, the second a matter of the heart. The first can leave us unchanged; the second intrinsically brings change.[1]

While women's wrestling has been truly surfacing in the last ten years or so, there still remains a sense of manliness to the frame of the sport. There's something about the element of combat—whether it be for fight or game—that screams of the role of a man. However, given the context of faith and the physical mirroring that I have alluded to, I can see the role of women being compatible with that of wrestlers. I'm sure they will be able to find relevance.

The question is not whether God cares about wrestling matches. I'm certain that He does, but not in terms of who wins or loses. He cares about wrestling matches to the extent that He cares about His creation using the gifts and talents that He has suffused in them. It's about taking what God has given you and purposing to use it to its fullest potential. It's about stepping on the mat and putting forth the utmost degree of effort in honor of the One who provided you with the ability to step on the mat in the first place. And furthermore, when your hand is raised in victory, it's about forgoing the glory and

---

[1]   Brennan Manning, The Ragamuffin Gospel (Colorado Springs, CO: Multnomah, 2005).

instead relinquishing it into the hands of the One who is truly glorious.

This subject (faith and wrestling) came about as a result of personal, theological reflection. There is a sense that aspects of life become illuminated as a result of faith's entry. In other words, when people embrace the God of the universe, that faith seems to reveal certain understandings that at one point were hidden in the darkness. This is not to say that people of faith are better, smarter, or have a superior intellect, but perhaps one of God's gifts to His followers is a little light that shines upon elements hidden within the darkness—a light which reveals how He is central to this whole story of life. As C. S. Lewis once stated, "I believe in Christianity as I believe that the sun has risen; not only because I see it, but because by it I see everything else."[2] I believe this rings true in relation to the experience of the Christian faith and potentially for the subject with which I have devoted this particular book.

---

[2] C.S. Lewis, *The Weight of Glory: And Other Addresses, revised edition* (San Fransisco, CA: HarperSanFrancisco, 1980).

CHAPTER 1

JACOB WRESTLES WITH GOD

B efore immediately jumping into the proceeding chapters, it's important to provide a bit of foundation and context to work with. Thankfully, the Bible contains an important story that does in fact provide this. In the book of Genesis, chapter 32, we find the story of Jacob wrestling with God (or an angel of the Lord). The story is a bit ambiguous about whom Jacob is actually wrestling with, but in some respects, the text appears to suggest that Jacob is wrestling with God Himself. Verse 30 has Jacob proclaiming, "I saw God face to face," and the book of Hosea makes reference to this same idea when the author writes, "As a man he struggled with God. He struggled with the angel and overcame him; he wept and begged for his favor" (Hosea 12:4). For the purposes of this book, we will, while respecting the ambiguous nature of the story, assume this suggestion.

In the chapters that follow, I will express both the nature and significance of an understanding of our relationship to God as Creator-creature. This story, however, will serve to pull us directly to the biblical text in order to provide a vivid picture with which to comprehend this, as well as the human struggle within it—the struggle that each individual goes through in submitting to this relationship and engaging it.

As human beings, we are drawn to stories. For the most part, we learn more effectively from them. They have the ability to make sense of something that otherwise might remain unclear. And given that this book is directed to a select group of individuals (wrestlers), what's more beneficial than a biblical story that discusses the very act of wrestling itself? What we extract from this narrative will provide key concepts that will be expanded upon throughout the course of this book. Moreover, the primary focus will be a deeper understanding of what it all means in light of one's role as a wrestler, and as one who claims to be a follower of Christ.

Now, for those familiar with the story, remember that this takes place during Jacob's journey back home (after an absence of many years) in order to reconcile with his brother, Esau. Jacob had done a grave injustice to Esau in essentially stealing God's blessing from their father, Isaac. This thievery, executed by Jacob, is particularly important to the analysis of this story.

Genesis 32:24–31 reads as follows:

> So Jacob was left alone, and a man wrestled with him till daybreak. When the man saw that he could not overpower him, he touched the socket of Jacob's hip so that his hip was wrenched as he wrestled with the man. Then the man said, "Let me go, for it is daybreak."
>
> But Jacob replied, "I will not let you go unless you bless me."
>
> The man asked him, "What is your name?"
>
> "Jacob," he answered.

Then the man said, "Your name will no longer be Jacob, but Israel, because you have struggled with God and with humans and have overcome."

Jacob said, "Please tell me your name."

But he replied, "Why do you ask my name?" Then he blessed him there.

So Jacob called the place Peniel, saying, "It is because I saw God face to face, and yet my life was spared."

The sun rose above him as he passed Peniel, and he was limping because of his hip.

A Challenge for Faith

The first thing one should notice is that while Jacob is wrestling with the man (potentially God in the form of an angel of the Lord), the man asks for his name in response to Jacob's demand for God's blessing. Jacob immediately declares, "Jacob," and his reply is followed by God's blessing. There are a few aspects that are significant about this question and response.

First, it relates back to the very deception performed by Jacob when accepting the blessing from his father. His father's eyes had grown weak from old age, and thus could not clearly see which of his sons he was placing God's blessing upon. So his father asked him, "Who is it?" to which Jacob responded, "I am Esau, your firstborn." What's even more interesting is that Isaac later asks him, before officially placing the blessing upon him, "Are you really my son Esau?" And Jacob replies, "I am."

So why is God asking Jacob for his name? Surely He already knows it. Well, the question, in one sense, is a challenge. Jacob's wrestling with God is not merely physical imagery of his inner struggle with himself and God (something that we will touch upon shortly), but it is also a pre-messianic (i.e. before Christ) confrontation (a gospel of sorts) that demands a response—an opportunity for Jacob to essentially *produce a response of faith*. Understanding the nature of this faith, given that it takes place prior to Christ, is a project that will not be pursued in this book. Though, in short, this is not far from the truth of the matter. Paul talks about the faith of Abraham in his letter to the Romans, and the author of the book of Hebrews does the same, along with identifying other key figures of the Old Testament in the subject of faith. Thus we can hold strongly to the notion that this encounter between Jacob and God is an encounter with the opportunity for faith to be born.

Wrestling

The physical wrestling that takes place within the question-and-response of this story is also incredibly important in and of itself. Jacob was wrestling with this question *internally*. Jacob desired reconciliation, not simply with his family and with God, but with himself as well. In part, he knew that the blessings of God represent a divine order in life and that this order represents a life put to rights, where human relationships are reconciled and where life itself is under the care and direction of God. Furthermore, Jacob wanted these blessings, and he wanted them on *his* terms. Every human being finds themselves in this struggle. Simply put, every human being, whether their life is filled with joy or hardship, finds themselves in a wrestling match with God. Humans are inherently inclined to seek life and refuge within themselves. They are inclined to hold onto authority, to try and sustain some manner of control when the subject is their life. And God graciously allows this wrestling to happen with the hope of producing faith. The truth of the matter is that life is not necessarily filled with endless joy. We are faced with the reality that, on this side of heaven, good and evil reside next to each other. And evil carries with it not just pain (which is terrible enough) but also uncertainty. Therefore, the question of authority becomes a question of how a person chooses to approach the uncertainty in life, or more specifically, in *their* life. Will the individual trust Christ in His remolding and shaping of their personhood? Will the individual *continue* to trust while walking through life and all the potential difficulty that might lie ahead? Or will they simply trudge along, dealing with matters within the context of their own power and authority?

Wrestling with an Injury

Now, what's interesting is that God impairs Jacob's hip in the very beginning of their wrestling match: "He touched the socket of Jacob's hip so that his hip was wrenched as he wrestled with the man" (verse 25). Thus Jacob was not merely wrestling with God. He was wrestling with an injury. But this did not stop him. It simply became another aspect within the context of his struggle with God. Again, and corresponding with what we pulled from the situation above, our wrestling with God takes place within a life that has been affected by evil. Therefore, many of us (if not all) have experienced some sort of pain in life. Pain becomes a part of us and our struggle with God. Pain is the dichotomy in our effort with Him. It both pulls us *away* from Him as well as draws us *to* Him. And when we choose to embrace God, the pain we have experienced turns into scars. God heals our pain, but the pain leaves its mark, and we do not forget it. The scars serve as a reminder of our commitment to Him. Just like a wedding ring reminds an individual of their promise of commitment to their spouse, so do our internal scars remind us of our need for, and commitment to, God. Remember that Jacob maintained his injury for the remainder of his life; and because of this, if ever he found himself forgetting, if ever he started to lose sight of who he was and of his confrontation with God, his scar (his injured hip) would remind him of his struggle and eventual decision to commit to God. Be careful, however, not to take this to say that I am suggesting that since God impairs Jacob's hip that God is the cause of evil. This is far from the truth, and far from the purpose of the above explication. The *imagery*, however, of pain in the midst of our struggle with God is the important element to acknowledge and understand.

New Creation

Also take note that upon Jacob's response, God changes his name. "Your name will no longer be Jacob, but Israel" (verse 28). This is a common theme throughout the biblical text. We see this sort of thing happen, for instance, with Abram becoming Abraham upon his faithful response to God's call on his life, which put into effect the divine plan of redemption. We later discover this is fulfilled in the life and resurrection of Jesus. And we see this in the New Testament with Saul becoming Paul upon his encounter with Christ on the road to Damascus; afterward, he becomes perhaps the greatest advocate and champion for the Christian faith who ever lived. This is not just a new name. This is a new identity. The New Testament teaches that when we embrace the gospel, we are a "new creation" in Christ (2 Corinthians 5:17). As stated earlier, it is my proposal that this confrontation between God and Jacob is a pre-messianic gospel. Jacob is given the opportunity to humble himself before God, to allow God to begin a new creation in him. When this happens, just as it occurs with those today who submit to the gospel of Jesus Christ, God begins a new creation in them. They are not the same person they were before. All the wonderful things that made up who they were prior to their encounter with Christ become infused with the glory and purposes of God. Essentially, God begins imparting the trueness of who they were always meant to be. This is the message intended when Jesus proclaims in the gospel narratives that, in dying to self, we gain life (Matthew 10:39; Luke 17:33; Mark 8:35). It is not merely a call to turn from a life of sin to a life of faith. It's a call to turn from (or die to) *our* understanding of our self, *our* self-infused purpose for our self. It's a call to surrender what *we* believe to be our true self for the *actual truth* as only God knows it. It's a promise that when we die to all this, we are actually given what we long for: our *true self.* Simply put, God holds this; and it is the desire of His heart to give it to us.

However, there's so much more to this promise of new creation. What takes place within the individual life is also happening on a much larger scale. God's plan of redemption (of new creation) is not distinctive to the lives of people. It involves the entirety of His creation. It is the desire of God to bring *all* His creation to rights, and He is doing just that. The gospel, therefore, is also the proclamation of a story that is taking place here and now and that which is moving along toward its fulfillment. Thus, the new creation that is taking place within each human being who surrenders to the gospel is intended to serve as a model, a display, of the new creation (a world put to rights) that is to come. We are invited *to be a part* of this, to be agents of that new creation here and now. Sin, therefore, is not a list of personal moral failings, but a rejection of this story being played out, a rejection to be a part of it, and thus a life that works *against* it. From a literal standpoint, *sin* (*hamartia* in Greek) is not so much "breaking the rules" as it is "missing the mark"; it's not simply the breaking of a law. It is the missing of an opportunity" (N. T. Wright).[3]

---

[3] N.T. Wright, *Simply Christian: Why Christianity Makes Sense* (New York, NY: HarperOne, 2006).

It is appropriate that in the same breath that sin and new creation are discussed, *repentance* finds its place. If we are to take this word literally as well, we come to find something that means a "change of mind" or a "change of direction" (from the Greek word *metanoia*). Repentance occurs when we see ourselves in light of Jesus' kingdom and realize the extent to which we have been living by a different system altogether. We realize, perhaps for the first time, how far we have fallen short of what we were made to be. Repentance, then, "is a serious turning away from patterns of life which deface and distort our genuine humanness" (N. T. Wright).[4]

The Initiation of God, Love, and True Humanness

A final aspect of the Jacob story that we cannot bypass relates to the *initiation of God*. If we return to this story, we find that it is God (not Jacob) who initiates this wrestling match. It is He who comes to Jacob. This is important in our understanding for two reasons. First, it is a proper understanding of faith as it truly exists, in that faith is not only a gift from God but it is also something in which He is always the source of instigation. It is not the human who walks through life and decides at some point or another, "I think I should reconcile my relationship with God." It is not the human who stops in their tracks and turns their direction toward God. It is always the case, when the subject is faith in the Christian God, that *He* approaches the *human*. And when contact is made, when the wrestling starts, it is the human who must react. Sometimes the wrestling lasts a lifetime. Sometimes faith is produced rather quickly and the remainder of the wrestling match becomes not so much a battle *for* or *against* a relationship with Him, but a battle in *deepening* a relationship with Him. Faith is thus a product of the individual's response to a confrontation initiated by God.

---

4   Wright, *Simply Christian: Why Christianity Makes Sense.*

Second, this action is distinct to the God of the Bible. It is a unique, divine characteristic found only in the Christian scriptures. It's a clearer understanding of His love for His creation. It is *love* that finds us in conflict with God. And it's not just that He invades our lives in order to bolster the possibility of a genuine relationship. It's that, in order to begin this relationship, He is willing to *wrestle* with us—not just wrestle for our hearts, but continue wrestling with us, after He has won our hearts, in order to sustain us and deepen that relationship. This is what Christianity has tried to define as *sanctification*—the work of God's Spirit (His Holy Spirit) in our lives in order to create a life more in harmony with the life perfected in Christ Jesus. For what Jesus Christ did was not merely reveal (in part) God Himself, not merely fulfill the divine plan to begin restoring a dying cosmos; He *revealed what it means to be human*. In other words, to follow Christ, to imitate Him, is to learn what it means to be authentically human as God intended.

Moving Forward

While we will surely discuss concepts that go beyond what has been revealed in this first chapter, the Jacob story will serve as a canvas (an *unfinished* canvas) for the discussion that awaits us in the following chapters.

So, what does all this mean for the Christian wrestler? The remainder of this book will serve not merely to answer this, but to exhort and encourage individuals who have assumed such a role, to take seriously what the meaning entails. We will do this by bringing to light those aspects of wrestling and faith that mirror each other.

CHAPTER 2

IT'S NOT ABOUT YOU

I t's not about you. And to be honest, this is a concept not
well-received, at least within the mind-set of the Western
world. In America specifically, there is this thriving notion
that people can pursue the American dream, the opportunity
to individually rise above the obstacles of life. Often, this is in
reference to some sort of quest toward financial success, which
carries with it the supposed opportunity for a better life. But
the term has evolved in its meaning. Living the American
dream has become the slogan for overcoming life's heavy
burdens and, not just setting personal goals of prosperity, but
ultimately seeing them emerge into reality. In the wrestling
world, Henry Cejudo was outspoken in his belief that he was
a product of the American dream when he won an Olympic
gold medal at the young age of twenty-one. He's the son of an
immigrant family who battled through the likes of poverty.
He's a prime example of what it looks like to individually rise
above the hardships of life and make something of oneself. But
is this really what life is all about? The question is not whether
we should desire to better ourselves and our situations. We
should. The question is in regard to the *focus* of this dream; and
the concern is that the American dream weighs heavy on the

scale of selfishness. The concern is that by focusing on ourselves we are, by default, disregarding others. Even more, the concern is that the American dream is distracting us from where our focus was intended to be: toward the direction of our Creator. And it's often the case that when we set our direction toward our Creator, He blesses that and encourages us to also orient ourselves toward others (Luke 10:27-28; Matthew 22:37; Mark 12:30-31). In other words, with God, it's the case that there are two avenues with which to set our sights on Him. One is to set our sights *directly* on Him through our time, thoughts, behavior, etc.; another is to do so *indirectly* through our treatment and service of others, and in so doing, we partially fulfill our role as ambassadors of God's new creation. Both lead to focusing on and honoring Him. Nevertheless, we're so consumed with ourselves and our own personal gain that *purpose* becomes a human invention as opposed to that which God provides.

Now, I don't know Henry Cejudo, and therefore can't say much about who he is as a person or if he is a man of faith. Regardless, his achievements are quite remarkable. All the above doesn't matter as much if faith isn't embodied in the individual in question. It's only when faith makes its entry that one's focus should be examined. Once an individual decides to trust and allow God to work in them (which is a primary aspect of what faith is) their focus becomes a shift from *I* to *Him*. The focus becomes a reversal from "all eyes on me" to "all eyes on God." This doesn't mean that the individual doesn't matter. It simply means that what makes up the identity and purpose of the individual is first and foremost of God. To put it in Christian terms, Christ becomes woven in and out of the fabric of their identity.

The Issue We Face

There was a former Catholic priest who described the problem of the modern man so eloquently. He wrote,

> Modern man is tempted to hope in himself. Surrounded by all the power now under his control, man today believes he can save himself. He resents dependence of any kind. Because he is able to transform the conditions of his life, he thinks he is able to transform himself and make himself the demiurge of the future. He trusts his own strength. He finds recourse to God repugnant. Besides, he sees God as an obstacle to his development. He thinks that he achieves his full stature only when he is his own highest value, and that humanism is only real when it denies God. Man believes he is self-sufficient.[5]

For a person of faith (and really for any person) this is an element of constant struggle. Ever since the Fall of man, humans have been inclined toward seeking refuge within themselves. It's an inclination that has us looking in the wrong direction. And because this has been our tendency since the event revealed in Genesis, humanity has come to believe that such a thing is normal. It's survival of the fittest, every man for himself. If man can't pull himself up by his own bootstraps, then perhaps he is altogether weak. Therefore, to fight against this is to fight against the norm.

Wrestling has that individual spotlight to it. When a match is won, it's because you won it. There's no such thing as a team effort when you shake hands with your opponent and prepare for battle. All the skill, strength, and energy put forth in that grueling match are performed by you and you alone. Other sports (more popular sports) have individuals *seeking* the spotlight. They must stand out among all the rest

---

[5] Jean Danie'lou, *The Christian Today*, translated by Kathryn Sullivan (New York, NY: Desclee Company, 1960).

in order to obtain their desired recognition. With wrestling, you don't have to seek. If you win enough matches and, in due course, win enough prestigious tournaments, the spotlight is unavoidable. As a result, the idea that "it's not all about me" can be difficult to acknowledge.

God's Icons

The Bible talks about humans as God's image bearers (*eikons* in Greek, or *icons* in English, i.e. Genesis 1:26–27). Among all God's creation, people are unique and set apart, bearing the mark of their Creator. Yet, at the same time, we're broken; for while we were beautifully and specially designed, we were also created to be in relationship with the One who created us. And in fact, to be separated from relationship with our Creator is to be separated from the fullness of our very being. When humans entered into the Fall, they lost a significant piece of their humanness, and it's only when they're reunited with God that they'll recapture it, or at least begin the process of reapplying that which was lost.

So here's the key: our primary objective is to make sure that we are in right relationship with our Creator. To be created is to be suffused with purpose. And since we are missing a crucial aspect of our humanity without God, a life in desperate search for fulfilling purpose and hope *apart* from Him is never truly found. Sure, we can find glimpses of purpose, but the nature of it is short-lived. C. S. Lewis, a renowned Christian author and apologist, though he did not coin the idea, often referred to this as "a God-shaped hole in the human heart." Humanity is not only left with emptiness, but it's an emptiness that can only be healed through divine intervention. Nevertheless, we tend to try and fill it apart from God through the likes of personal and public accolades, money, sex, and alcohol, or we even seek fulfillment in others, specifically through relationships. We, for instance, think that a significant other has the ability to fill our deepest needs and desires. The problem is that they are broken too. They too are left with divine emptiness, and they too are seeking the same fulfillment from us. As a result, we are often left disappointed. Yet when we embrace the God of the Bible, we discover this emptiness beginning to be filled. This does not mean that the emptiness discovers its complete fulfillment in the present life, but that it has begun to be sufficiently filled by God Himself and that He is working in us toward the complete satisfaction of which we long for, and of which we will fully realize in the life to come.

The Creator

As wrestlers, the above may apply as far as the different methods in which we try to fill our emptiness, but we also add an element. We become gladiators in pursuit of our own freedom. Success on the mat becomes our leading destiny. Championships become the means by which to feed our identity. We absorb the praise and forget the One who provided us the very gifts and talents that we put into action. We feed the illusion that we're our own creators, that we built ourselves from the ground up out of nothing.

The One who "creates out of nothing" (i.e. *creatio ex nihilo*) is, and only is, God Himself. So even in the act or pursuit of being creators (or specifically, creators out of nothing) we are in a pursuit of something that is, by its very nature, divine. We are in pursuit of being godlike, or God Himself. We are single handedly attempting to reverse the intended composition of the relationship between God and human. Instead of recognizing ourselves as creature and God as Creator, we try to do away with our role as creature and assume the role of creator. In so doing, we place ourselves on the same level as God or do away with Him altogether. And this is attempted both consciously and unconsciously. Some people know full well what they are doing, while others are simply doing so as a result of their inherited sinful nature. They may not necessarily recognize their pursuit for what it is, but regardless, they are tampering with their relationship with God.

This is a crucial aspect of the Christian gospel. The gospel, among other things, awakens people to their relationship with God.

The gospel reestablishes the relationship between God and human. When people accept it, they are, in part, recognizing their role in the divine relationship—their role as creature and God as Creator. Furthermore, when people have embraced the gospel, they have also chosen to exemplify this role in every aspect of their lives. They are advocates for the new creation, the true and pervasive story that God is at work in completing. This means that every time, for instance, a wrestler steps on the mat, the mind-set is not merely to *win* (though the desire to win is certainly good) but to wrestle with a sense of purpose in competing to glorify God. Put simply, the wrestler's mind-set corresponds with putting into action that which God has given. Wrestling then becomes a form of worship.

If winning is the mind-set, then winning becomes the focus. But there can only be one focus. We were not designed with the ability to whole-heartedly focus on multiple things at once. We were designed with the ability to fully focus on one thing and one thing only. Why? Because it takes sacrifice; because when your focus is on God then your focus is not on yourself. The question following the match is not, "Did I win?" The question is, "Did I give it my all? Was God satisfied with my effort?" You see, ultimately, it's not about winning or losing, but wrestling for an audience of one and hoping that He's pleased with your performance. Olympic champion Jordan Burroughs put it this way in a blog he published on December 21, 2012: "Winning and losing isn't always what's important. Performing at your highest level is. When you let the thought of winning and losing affect your performance, you allow your ego to affect you negatively. When you focus on performing at your highest level, the winning takes care of itself."

And here's the thing: one can easily decipher a wrestler's focus. It's not something that can be hidden. How they discuss their objective (their focus) gives clear insight into how they recognize their role as a creature and as a wrestler.

When a wrestler is interviewed after a championship match, they have one of two options: they can absorb the glory, or they can redirect it to where it's truly deserved. And, again, to do this is to fight against ourselves. We *want* the glory. We *want* the praise. To redirect it away from ourselves, especially after accomplishing something extraordinary, is perhaps the most unnatural objective one could conjure up in that situation. But regardless, and despite that it might produce an unnatural feeling, it's what we are called to do. We are called to exemplify our role in the divine relationship and the divine story of redemption. Wherever we are, no matter the circumstance, we are called to reveal our role as creature in order to direct the eyes of others to the Creator.

CHAPTER 3

TRANSFORMING WRESTLING FROM IDOL TO ICON

We have this tendency to think we can claim ownership over things— that whatever we have or possess is something that is in our immediate control. The result is that when we think about those things that we *possess*, we fail to look beyond ourselves. And not only is it a lie to believe that we can claim true ownership over anything, but the notion is a distraction from the purpose of the thing itself. The things of this world—anything that is good and effectual in an individual's life—are designed to be a means by which to be reminded of God. For example, when one thinks about their possessions—house, car, job, etc.—he or she should immediately be reminded of God and look to Him, because "every good and perfect gift is from above" (James 1:17). These things were designed by God to serve as *icons* pointing to Himself. They were designed to cause the human being to look beyond themselves and to fixate on God—to be reminded of His ever-flowing sovereignty and presence. The famous A. W. Tozer once wrote,

> There is within the human heart a tough fibrous root of fallen life whose nature is to possess, always to possess ... Things have become necessary to us, a development never originally intended. God's gifts now take the place of God, and the whole course of nature is upset by the monstrous substitution.[6]

Part of sin's influence in our lives is this very issue: the belief that we have, or can acquire, possession or control over certain things, that we have the ability to claim ownership over them. The issue is that once we've given into this belief then we've also given into the idea that we are not fully dependent on God. It's the absurd belief that we are, in some respects, self-sustaining or self-existent. And yet, it's the Christian belief that God, and only God, is truly such. Moreover, there's also the understanding that, in creating, God established Himself as *necessary* for the continuation of His creation's existence. Put simply, God, in the act of creating, established a covenant with Himself as the Creator and therefore sustainer of creation. Our very existence is dependent on God upholding it. Apart from Him, we do not exist.

Therefore, as it pertains to wrestling, it is not our possession. We cannot claim ownership over it. We are merely accepting and putting into action what God has provided. Wrestling is not something for us to claim, but a blessing in which to engage. This means that we, in our wrestling, strive to be the best, push ourselves to the limits, make the necessary sacrifices; but in the end, we relinquish ownership of the thing itself to Him. Furthermore, when we look upon the sport and our involvement in it, we look beyond ourselves and allow

---

[6]   A. W. Tozer, *The Pursuit of God*, Tozer Legacy Edition (Camp Hill, PA: Christian Publications, Inc., 1982).

wrestling itself to be an icon that points to God. As a result, and when we allow it to produce its divinely intended purpose, we then respond with gratitude. We thank Him for allowing us to participate in the sport. We thank Him for allowing us the opportunity to push our mind, body, and spirit to their utmost potential. We thank Him for allowing us to involve ourselves in something that is, at its core, an opportunity to worship Him.

What we don't want to do is allow something to become an idol: something that takes the place of God as our focus and source of worship. An icon is very different from an idol, in that the thoughts that transpire head in two different directions. Again, when something is viewed as an icon, the thing is pointing beyond itself and toward the direction of God. However, when something is viewed as an idol, the thoughts remain with the thing itself; and as a result, the *thing* becomes the focus and source of our worship. Wrestling must not be seen in light of idol worship. Wrestling and all that is occupied with it is not the goal; the goal is Christ. The goal is always to utilize what is available to us in order to direct our eyes, and the eyes of others, toward God Himself.

Nate Toedter

Nate Toedter came from a rather large family in rural Minnesota, the middle child with four siblings on either side of him. He was raised in what could be described as a Christian home, and therefore was introduced to the gospel at a young age. The beliefs and values he inherited were always integral to his life, and as a result, he never chose to rebel like so many young people do at some point or another. Nevertheless, wrestling became a source of personal value. For him, wrestling was a measuring stick, a way to determine self-worth. Put simply, success on the mat was what provided him value as a human being.

Nate started wrestling as a sophomore in high school; and because he entered the sport a bit later than most, he was always playing catch-up. The first couple years proved to be more of an introduction, figuring out of how to wrestle in the first place, learning what it takes to win matches. However, by his senior year, Nate was already setting himself up for success. Winning was now an expectation; and all he could think about was winning a state title. If he accomplished that goal, according to his measuring stick formula, it meant he was worth something.

His goal, however, was shot down quickly when he lost in the state quarterfinals by a narrow score of 4–2. Having already envisioned standing on top of the podium, a championship medal around his neck, Nate was devastated by the loss. In his mind, he was far more skilled and talented. He trained harder than any opponent who stepped on the mat with him. After two hours under the bleachers, tears shed and body still sick with disappointment, he decided right then and there that he was going to wrestle in college and that he was going to be a national champion. Not because of potential delight in the accomplishment itself, but because the accomplishment would perhaps give him the self-worth he was unable to achieve in high school.

Nate went on to wrestle at St. Cloud State University in Minnesota, a Division II school in athletics. By his junior year, it looked as if he was prepped and ready to win a national championship. He was in great shape, healthy, had the best record in the nation coming into the national tournament, and had already beaten (at some point during the season) the opponents who appeared on his side of the bracket. But during his first match, he tore the ligaments in his thumb. He lost that match and was forced to wrestle the remainder of the tournament with a club for a hand, his forearm and hand thoroughly wrapped and taped in order to immobilize his thumb. He ended up taking seventh place in the tournament, a repeat of his performance the previous year. The disappointment fueled him into his final season. He rehabbed, stayed healthy, and trained harder than he ever had before. There wasn't a shadow of a doubt that Nate Toedter was going to be a national champion.

His first two matches in the national tournament reflected a story that was common throughout his senior season: that of winning and doing so decisively. However, when he reached the semifinals, he found himself in an unexpected a battle, one that had him once again on the losing end. He lost by a close score of 9–8, and immediately everything came crashing down around him. The self-worth he had strived for was now out of reach. He hadn't won a state championship, and that was followed by a failed campaign for a national championship. Moreover, failure to win a Division II national championship ousted him from being able to compete on wrestling's biggest stage: the Division I national tournament. Back then, the top competitors in each of the lower divisions qualified to compete at the Division I tournament: a chance to become an All-American or even win an elusive national championship. Despite the loss, Nate continued the tournament and proceeded to capture third place.

Sitting on the bleachers following the completion of the tournament, numb from the weight of defeat and thinking that he had wasted so many years of his life training in the sport, God grabbed his attention. Like a strong yet subtle voice, God spoke to him. "You're going to the Division I tournament. Not because of anything you did to earn it, but because I want you there."

Nate hadn't paid much attention to the rules or criteria for how one was bolstered into the tournament, but he knew one thing for sure: "I'm third place. No third place guy goes. So

I don't know how you're going to work that out." The notion didn't even excite him. He slumped over and tried his best to ignore it.

It was in that moment that Nate's coach came walking through the gymnasium doors with a big smile on his face. "What are you smiling about?" Nate asked him.

"You're going to the D1s!" his coach said with excitement. "Every coach picked you as their first vote. They could pick five wildcards to go to the tournament. You got every coach's vote to go first!"

Nate went to the 1989 NCAA Division I tournament; but this time, he wasn't driven by his own agenda. He was there because he believed God wanted him there. The burden of success was taken off his shoulders. For the first time, he was able to wrestle with freedom. Rather than wrestle with deep-seated worry and stress about winning, rather than being driven by his measuring stick of self-worth, Nate actually had fun! He was competing for God, as if he was wrestling for God's enjoyment. Nate Toedter achieved Division I All-American honors.

Prior to God stepping in, Nate had tried to force wrestling to work for him on *his* terms. He used it to produce a certain measure of worth as a human being. Wrestling was about him. But God, in a sense, took it from him. The sport could never do for Nate what he wanted it to. And God didn't just take it from him, He gave it back. But He did so with a clear understanding of the terms by which it was given: His terms. God made it clear that He is bigger than wrestling. Wrestling, if used as a measuring stick of self-worth, will never truly suffice. For even if an individual achieves his goals in the sport, how long does the self-worth assumed truly last? How long until it wears off? God alone holds the abundance of this measure, and this self-worth can neither be earned nor achieved. Moreover, God made it clear to Nate that He *wanted* him to wrestle. He enjoyed watching him compete in the sport. Nate transformed wrestling from idol to icon. He was *worshiping* God through his wrestling.

A New Objective

As indicated in the previous chapter, wrestling is not about you. It's about something far greater than you. And those who have genuinely considered this are, for the most part, those who discover the most freedom in wrestling, because the burden of success is no longer one that they must bear; success becomes redefined. Winning is no longer the primary objective, though it remains important. The primary objective becomes a pursuit of God's pleasure; it's an objective that is fulfilled when and if wrestlers rise to the challenge of putting everything they have on the mat, every time they step foot on it. God *wants* us to compete! He *wants* us to expel every last shred of energy we can to win a match! And it's only when we strive for success, only when we put forth everything we have in utilizing the gifts and talents God has given us that He is pleased. He passionately desires for us to use what He has given and attempt to exhaust it! The amazing thing is that we *can't* truly exhaust it! We can forever seek to better ourselves in whatever area God has blessed us. And God has blessed a lot of people with gifts and talents that pervade several different areas in life.

CHAPTER 4

IT'S A LIFESTYLE

I n other sports, there is the ability to compartmentalize the training in conjunction with other aspects of life. The task seems a bit easier. This is not to say that one can't successfully compartmentalize wrestling to some degree, but if a wrestler truly desires to be great in the sport—and to be great should be a desire; no one dreams of being mediocre—then there is the inevitable force of the sport influencing every other facet of their life. In fact, one could even go so far as to say that it is *required* that the sport have this type of force; for you can't be as successful if you do not allow it to be so. And once you allow it to impact your life, the change is gradual but obvious. It takes a great deal of commitment, but the results become not only apparent to yourself but to others as well.

Faith can be seen in the same light—even more so, really. There's no such thing as a Christian whose faith doesn't require complete focus and commitment. Sure, anyone can claim the title, but what sort of influence does it carry in their life? Does it change their course in a significant way? Does it cause them to interact with people differently? Does it force them to approach the world differently than if they weren't a person of faith? The evidence of faith is visible. As much as we may try and make it something hidden or private, it's not. If it's not visible, then it's most likely nonexistent; real, genuine faith calls us to action. If we are not influenced to live differently on account of our faith then we are calling on some sort of silent faith, a faith that really isn't faith at all.

There's the notion that faith works like magic, that once you engage in life with Christ, your life is changed in an instant. However, this notion is filled with emptiness. God isn't a magician, and the change doesn't necessarily make life full of endless joy (though there is joy in Christ, but a kind far different than the joy we identify as such in this life). God is a life-changer, and the only true life-changer. Such work is not instantaneous, even for God. It certainly could be, but that would dismiss the actual goal in mind. You see, the goal is to change you from the inside out, which requires your dedication and commitment. It requires reciprocation. And yet, the problem is that our ability to reciprocate is often distracted. We find ourselves caught up in other things, things that pull us away from a push forward to faithful living. Therefore, while God is working to mold and shape us into the human beings we were intended to be, He is also doing so *in* and *through* us. In other words, He has graciously committed Himself to us in our constant state of misguidance and failures. He is committed to us even when we aren't moving forward, even when we are altogether stagnant and perhaps stranded.

And while the change is a gradual one, it is also an evident one. God's work in a person is not designed to go unnoticed. If God is at work in an individual, it will be seen. Others will take notice of the change that occurs. They will take notice of the choices you make, and the way in which you approach the world. They will notice your failures as well. Not because they are identifiers of who you are, but because they have become a contrast to who you have become and are becoming.

To allow something to consume you, it needs to pervade the framework of your identity. It needs to affect you in a way that the choices you make are a product of it. For instance, and especially in the midst of the competitive season, a wrestler meticulously chooses to do and not do certain things. They avoid those things that do not serve to sustain the health of their body, whether it's related to diet, certain social activities, drugs, etc. And while a wrestler avoids these things to protect their physical nature, the Christian avoids these things in protection of their spiritual nature; for the Christian wrestler, both aspects are at work. In essence, they are training their body for battle.

Faith in Training

In the early movement of Christianity, the idea of training your body for spiritual battle was a deep characteristic of the faith. Those who truly devoted themselves to this practice were known as *ascetics*. Asceticism comes from the Greek word *askesis*, which literally means "exercise" or "training." Those committed to this way of life remained abstinent from worldly pleasures and instead devoted themselves to continuous prayer and fasting. The vast majority of Christians in the early stages of the movement were ascetic (particularly the growing church in the East). In short, to be a Christian was to live a life of asceticism. And thus, to partake in the lifestyle of Christianity was to willingly engage in battle with the evil spiritual forces that permeate the world, and to willingly engage in the training that would prepare one to enter into these anticipated situations—and to do so on the world's behalf.

To be a Christian was far from a lackadaisical choice. It involved a commitment that proved to be a radical reorientation in living. Put simply, it was impossible for faith to remain a backdrop in your life. If it didn't change you and your overall focus, then it was hardly an authentic step into Christianity at all. This redirection in life and focus was a requirement. It was a visible and powerful product of faith itself. It was evidence of God's work in the life of a human.

Now, this is not to say that we become Christian ascetics in the sense that we completely separate ourselves from the world and that we devote all our time and energy to prayer and fasting. But it does mean that we become Christian ascetics in the sense that we take up the idea that we are to exercise or train ourselves in the faith. Christianity is a way of life, and in many ways, so is wrestling. Understanding this is paramount to moving in a positive direction as a Christian, as a wrestler, and as a Christian wrestler.

Costly Grace

Let's take this further. To be a successful wrestler, it costs something. It costs your time, energy, and, to some extent, your life. It requires sacrifice. There is a very real sense of change in life; for in order to move in a positive direction as a wrestler, one must forego a way of life that would hinder one's progress. And for the most part, those things involved in that other way of life are hard to let go of. For instance, one's social life is very much an important and cherished element (and, for the most part, good). However, it's fair to say that *it will* be affected. The time (and extra time) needed in order to be successful in the sport means less time is available to partake in social situations and events. And while it is certainly possible to incorporate a healthy social life, this area, without a doubt, will be directly impacted by the time spent training as a wrestler.

Even more than the sacrifice of letting go of certain things, it's also about *enacting* things. It's about that which is involved proactively in one's training—putting one's body through strenuous labor in order to prepare it for competition; and not simply the body, but the mind and spirit as well. You force every part of you to be pushed to its limits. Or you even suppress the idea that such limits exist and instead force every part of you to be pushed further and further every day. You sacrifice rest and comfort.

Yet while the sacrifice is hard, and certainly has the capability to wear on an individual, most would say that the sacrifice is worthwhile because it is done with purpose. The sacrifice is implemented with the understanding that it is aligned with intention and meaning. There is a goal in mind that a wrestler is striving for. There is a place, a hope, that awaits them upon the completion of their training, a place that demands preparation. Quite simply, there are battles that await them, battles that would consume and overtake them had they not devoted themselves to the necessary sacrifices and training.

We must recognize that faith is parallel with the above, and to a level that far exceeds it. For though we are saved by the grace of God, it is a costly grace, a grace that demands sacrifice; it demands that the individual accepting the grace of God surrender his or her life and will to the Giver of grace. This requires a step away from a life of sin and into a life of grace. The problem is that sin is not easy to step away from. It is disguised with beauty—a false beauty, but beauty nonetheless. In fact, to step away from certain areas of sin can be painful, because much of sin is a life that involves one's own desires and will. It's a life of freedom for the individual, but a freedom that leads to destruction. It's a freedom that ultimately leads to a rejection of life itself. For if the only way in which to regain the fullness of our being is through Christ, and in so doing the Creator-creature relationship is reestablished in a way that the creature is given something valuable (true humanness), then to reject God is to reject human life; because human life was never intended to exist apart from relationship with the

Creator. In other words, to refuse relationship with God is to fold back into nothing, to willingly embrace the destination to which sin leads: death. But again, this sinful beauty, this free life of human will, is difficult to walk away from. For to engage life in Christ is to surrender this will, to forego it, and to instead embrace a life that demands full obedience to the will and freedom of God. And yet, this human sacrifice is not in vain. It's a life aided by the power of God, and it comes with abundance and a freedom that leads to life everlasting! Life in obedience to God is authentic human living!

Freedom That Is Here, but Not Yet

As followers of Christ, as receivers of this costly grace, we are nevertheless stuck in a present existence in which the true nature and fullness of this freedom in God is not yet experienced. It is the goal that awaits us. It is that which we strive for. And because of this, we are living as those who presently live in God's freedom, but who also must combat the life of sin on a daily basis. The life that leads to destruction still affects us, though it no longer has a hold on us. It is no longer the direction in which we are headed, but it nonetheless still has the capability to influence us and cause us to stumble.

Fortunately, once one engages Christ, Christ enters into the human life. He becomes that which allows obedience to God to be possible. Through His Spirit, God begins pushing us along the road that leads to everlasting life. He begins pulling us to Himself.

CHAPTER 5

IT'S A BATTLE

Wrestling is a battle. Of all the chapters within this book, the content within this one might ring most true. Wrestling, by definition, refers to struggle. To the ancient Greeks, wrestling was regarded as the best expression of strength among all other competitions. Just like in the Jacob story discussed in the first chapter, wrestling is a physical mirroring of the wrestling (the battle) that takes place within the spiritual nature of any given human being. We're wrestling with God at times, and we're also wrestling with the evil that is attempting to overcome us on a spiritual level. We're in a battle for our self as well as for the church.

The scriptures tell us that "our struggle is not against flesh and blood, but against the rulers, against the authorities, against the powers of this dark world and against the spiritual forces of evil in the heavenly realms" (Ephesians 6:12). And before and after this explanation is a call to arms. The scriptures literally tell us to "put on the full armor of God" (Ephesians 6:11, 13). As Christians enraptured in the culture of the modern West, we can often find ourselves losing sight of this crucial element of the faith. Furthermore, we can become so captivated with the notion of God's love that we forget or ignore the suggestion that we are in the midst of a war. According to this particular chapter in the book of Ephesians, and that which is supported throughout the biblical text, the way in which we combat the evil forces of this world is through obedience to God's will in the course of our thoughts and behavior, as well as through prayer. This means that contrary to what many modern pastors have suggested, prayer is not merely a practice in which the person executing the prayer is changing into a more God-centered human being. This is only partly true. Prayer is also a resource for military means, a spiritual weapon. Pastor and theologian Greg Boyd, whether you agree with his theological opinions or not, has been a pioneer in the discussion of spiritual warfare. He has done a great deal in encouraging the church to take spiritual matters more seriously. If nothing more, Boyd has almost single-handedly encouraged Christians to consider taking a more active role in their faith.

Just as in life and in matters of the Christian faith, the sport of wrestling consists of many battles, those that contain ups and downs, triumphs and defeat. These battles can be short or long. They can be tiresome, filled with disappointment, or produce feelings and an outcome of victory. Through it all is the life of a warrior who continues the march forward. Through it all is the warrior becoming stronger, wiser, and more courageous. No matter what, they continue chasing victory.

Jack Spates

When Jack Spates engaged in a debate with a young Christian couple regarding Jesus, he found himself at a loss. He was twenty years old, taking a redshirt year away from college competition, and had just arrived at an open tournament in Maryland with a friend to get in some mat time. (Taking a redshirt year doesn't necessarily mean that a wrestler ceases to compete altogether.) Any argument he lofted at them was immediately refuted by a statement by Jesus found in the gospels. In short, Jack found it difficult to argue about Jesus … with Jesus. The debate was rather strange for him too, in that, in some respects, he considered himself a Christian, at least in the cultural sense of the term. He grew up going to Catholic school, and up until fifteen years of age, he and his family were consistent church-going members.

The debate he found himself in while in Maryland stuck with him as he made his way back to Slippery Rock University. In an odd way, the subject of Jesus and the Christian faith seemed to be following him wherever he went. Prior to leaving for the tournament, Jack walked into a dorm room and found himself awkwardly walking into a group of people having a Bible study. They asked him to stay, but he wanted nothing to do with the ordeal, turned around, and tried to pretend like it never happened.

While he tried his best to ignore the prodding on his heart to take faith more seriously, he couldn't. Jack ended up joining a Bible study shortly after his return to campus, and surrendered his life to Christ.

Jack's conversion came within the confines of a more legalistic persuasion of the faith, and the consequences of that initiated a battle that would continue for many years to follow. You see, his heart was God's, but, in a sense, his mind was elsewhere. In other words, while his engagement with the faith was genuine, his mind was still partly captive to the Evil One. Legalism is, for a lack of better terms, a nasty perversion with which the Evil One (Satan)—or his counterparts—has a way into the mind of the believer. This open door into the believer's mind allows him the opportunity to cause the Christian to stumble. In short, legalism views the Christian faith as a system of moral rights and wrongs. It's more concerned with the list (the system) than it is with the heart. This is not to say that legalistic Christians lack authenticity in their pursuit of God.

It simply means that their minds are clouded from seeing the big picture.

As a result of Jack's newfound Christian faith, he discovered himself in a constant struggle; he was outspoken regarding his faith, using his platform as a wrestler, but inside he was battling with sin. He was battling with the legalistic frame of mind, which embodied a good portion of his Christian worldview. So much so, that Jesus' words in the gospels of "giving rest" and an assurance of an "easy yoke" and a "light burden" only caused confusion. *Easy burden? Yeah right!* he would think to himself. *This is hard!* Though he discovered life in Christ, there also seemed to be life in the secular world, which he was restricted from partaking in.

Jack married during his junior year, and after a successful college wrestling campaign, which included a NCAA national championship and NCAA runner-up finish the following year, he sought to find some peace from the spiritual war that was taking him over. Contrary to how most go about searching for answers, Jack enrolled in seminary. He learned of a seminary close by where he could coach wrestling alongside his studies.

His first class at Baptist Bible College and Seminary caught him completely off guard. He took an Old Testament course and realized just how far behind he was compared with many of the other students. He didn't even know the books of the Bible, let alone could he provide a successful approach of biblical criticism and theology. Yet while he struggled, and even took a year off to recuperate, Jack earned his Master of Divinity and developed a good start to his career as a wrestling coach in the process.

Following his years in seminary, he spent a short time as a youth pastor. Afterwards he tried his hand in the business world. Unfortunately, the tension in his mind never settled in regard to his faith.

Amid all of this, he returned to various coaching jobs. He coached at Pittsburgh, West Point, and Cornell prior to taking over a struggling Oklahoma University wrestling program. Jack had built a solid reputation for himself as a wrestling coach, and the experience and accolades eventually swallowed his focus. No longer was he as concerned with his spiritual battle with legalism or an immediate focus on his faith. Instead, he found worth and satisfaction in the arena of coaching wrestling: building programs complete with All-Americans, national champions, and a name for himself as an altogether great coach. Instead of fighting the battle with the evil forces behind legalism and searching for comfort in his faith, he gave in. And for the next seventeen years of his life, Jack would discover the darkness that ensues with the walk away from a loving and gracious God.

Jack's departure from God and into the arms of sin had his life change dramatically. Though he was accomplishing great things as a wrestling coach and increasing in stature in terms of his abilities to develop a strong program, he was decreasing in fulfillment with some of the more important aspects in life. Jack had all he ever wanted, but he was growing progressively more empty. His new course in life saw tremendous turmoil in his life, and the weight of his struggle began to overwhelm him. He had allowed sin to caress him. It felt good, and it ultimately grabbed him. Jack eventually reached a point where he didn't want to leave. He was essentially a slave to it, though the slavery was in his unwillingness to find freedom. He was in so deep he didn't know where to begin to crawl back even if he wanted to.

Jack had basically accepted his situation in life as unalterable. And when recruiting a young man whose parents had a sincere desire for their son to wrestle for Jack and Oklahoma University due to remembering Jack's outspoken Christian faith during his early coaching years, he wanted to start being honest about where he was at. When the conversation turned toward faith, Jack politely said to the young recruit, "Look, I don't want you to come here on false pretenses, and I certainly don't want to lie to you. I'm not walking with the Lord. In fact, I can't even say I'm a Christian." That wrestler, after following up with his parents, decided to pursue his wrestling career elsewhere.

Years continued to pass, and Jack was falling deeper and deeper into emptiness. He experienced a serious health issue, though surprisingly, the fearful reminder of death didn't cause him to change his course. It merely gave him an element of gratitude to be alive. It wasn't until Jack began to truly see his present circumstance in life—feeling the immense burden of his loneliness—that he realized he had to at least try and turn things around. He started to pray, read his Bible, and at some point or another, he walked into a church. Eventually, he began to talk about his life with a pastor. He opened up his heart, and allowed himself to be vulnerable. He told the pastor how long he had walked away from Lord and what he had done throughout the course of his departure from the arms of God. Jack felt that he had wasted so many years running away that he didn't even know where he stood in the eyes of God. He was confused. His decision to follow Jesus so many years ago was genuine; but by no means was he following Him. So what did that mean? He felt that perhaps he was a lost cause. He didn't believe that he really knew God, and maybe God didn't even want to know *him*. But the pastor graciously, and with sincere conviction, began to quote a verse from Second Peter. "Jack," he said, "what you need to understand is that although seventeen years seems like forever to you, it's only a moment for God. With the Lord, a day is like a thousand years and a thousand years are like a day." As the pastor began to quote Second Peter, Jack started to weep. "Jack," he continued, "all is not lost. God still loves you. Though you have walked away for a time, He is a God of endless grace and love, and I am certain that He awaits you with open arms."

This was a turning point for Jack. God embraced him with love and began mending his broken and repentant heart. Jack shared his experience with his family and asked for forgiveness for all the pain that he had caused them. Jack was the prodigal son who had finally made his way back home into the warm embrace of his loving Father.

About six months after his return to the Lord, Jack was sharing his story with an old teammate in the stands at the annual high school national tournament. As he told his story (the story of his departure and return to God), a young man shot up from behind them. The abrupt movement caught the attention of Jack and his friend. Both staring at him, the young man said with a look of shock, "Jack, about seven years ago you were recruiting me to wrestle at Oklahoma. You were honest with me about where you were in life and about your walk away from the Lord. Jack ... my mom has been praying for you this whole time!" It was in that moment Jack realized that even though he had walked away, even though he had surrendered the battle for his faith seventeen years ago, somewhere along the way, someone else stepped in and fought his battle for him. This woman, whom he had never met, had been praying and engaging in spiritual warfare on his behalf for seven years! And once Jack made his return, he stepped back onto the battlefield and faced his foe head on.

After years of success as a wrestling coach at Oklahoma, Jack felt God calling him in another direction. Though many years had passed, God was ready to pick up where he had left off with Jack. In 2011, he stepped down as head coach at Oklahoma University and took a step into Christian ministry. In regard to his battle with legalism, it's a battle he has won. As a result, he can more clearly see the meaning and purpose of Jesus' call to follow Him. Moreover, the words of Jesus, which promise an "easy yoke" and a "light burden," are no longer met with confusion but instead met with understanding and joy.

The Thief in Disguise

Legalism has been a long lasting entryway for the Evil One and his counterparts. In fact, when Jesus engages the Pharisees in the gospel narratives, He spends a great deal of His time refuting legalism and the sin that transpires from it. He accuses the Pharisees time and time again of being so enamored with the Torah (Jewish law) that they have completely lost sight of the heart of the matter. Instead of concerning themselves with the meaning and purpose of the Torah, they became overly concerned with Torah itself. In other words, instead of being infatuated with the Law Giver (God), they became infatuated with the Law alone. And the Pharisees even took it a step further in using the Law to bolster a sense of moral elitism, which had them essentially praising themselves for their *own* righteousness as opposed to the righteousness of God. Legalism, though at times well intentioned, is a thief in disguise.

No Easy Mission

Though the issue of legalism contains within it a tie to many sins, the spiritual battles we face pervade several other areas as well. In fact, sexual sin alone is a battle that, for many men, carries the most pressing force. The difficulty with sin is that it can be ambiguously luminous. So much of it is tied to the normal and even necessary facets of society and culture that it can actually appear to be *life-giving*. But what most come to find is that although it *appears* to be life-giving, the life it gives is short and simply serves as a means to push them toward another potential life-giving sin, until they are so steeped in sin that they completely lose sight of where they're going or even how to get back to where they once were.

The mission of the individual Christian, and the church as a whole, is no easy one. We are sinners saved by grace. As stated in the previous chapter, this means that we are, in this present life, stuck in a situation in which sin still has the ability to affect our lives. We are just as much a sinner as the unbeliever is. The only difference between the believer and the unbeliever is the mere fact that the believer has surrendered to the Holy Spirit's tug on their heart, has accepted God's gift of grace, and allowed God to begin His work in their life in order to change them into a person more reflective of His image. The believer has essentially allowed God to begin restoring the distorted image of Himself that they possess through the process of cleaning them up, putting their broken pieces back together, and breathing new life into them. The unbeliever, on the other hand, has had no part in allowing God to do this work in their life, and has furthermore found contentment in their life as it is.

The sport of wrestling mirrors the often-tiresome wrestling battles each human being faces on a spiritual level. And in a lot of ways, a wrestler is able to actually approach these battles with more strength and conviction because they can appropriate it to what they have experienced on a physical level. To some degree, a wrestler knows what it's like to engage in war.

CHAPTER 6

WRESTLING AND THE HUMAN EXPERIENCE

O ne of the most interesting realizations an individual can discover is the truth that wrestling is a significant part of the human experience. Struggle, temptation, suffering, and the wrestling we must do with them, are a part of the human predicament. The previous chapter brought to light the notion of spiritual warfare and the battles that ensue for the individual Christian life and the church as a whole. But the concept goes beyond one's practice as a Christian. Wrestling is simply a part of what it means to be a human being, at least on this side of heaven. It's a component of what makes a person real and authentic. Any life outside the realm of struggle, temptation, and/or suffering is a life that is essentially out of touch with humanity.

Jesus the Wrestler: The Temptation Story

When considering Jesus, His wrestling abilities aren't exactly a part of the thought process. But truth be told, Jesus, within the context of wrestling with the fallen aspects of life, was the greatest wrestler of all time. One theologian puts it like this:

> Jesus suffers the full consequences of evil: evil from the political, social, cultural, personal, moral, religious and spiritual angles all rolled into one; evil in the downward spiral hurtling toward the pit of destruction and despair. And he does so precisely as the act of redemption, of taking that downward fall and exhausting it, so that there may be new creation, new covenant, forgiveness, freedom and hope (N. T. Wright).[7]

Jesus, through his life, death, and resurrection, took upon Himself the entirety of human suffering, and made a spectacle of it on the cross.

From a Christian perspective, we know that wrestling is an authentic expression of humanity, partially because of the temptation story in the gospels. This segment of Jesus' story precedes His mission to the cross and His subsequent resurrection from the dead.

Evangelical Christians are often guilty of emphasizing Jesus' divinity so much that they lose sight of His humanity. Jesus was perfectly God and yet perfectly human. If we lose sight of His human nature, we essentially lose sight of our immediate connection to Him. The writers of the gospels (specifically, Matthew, Mark, and Luke), were very intentional when including the temptation story within their explication

---

[7]   N.T. Wright, *Evil and the Justice of God* (Downers Grove, IL: InterVarsity Press, 2006).

of Jesus' life and mission. The inclusion of this story answers several questions that run through people's minds.

Now, if you're a biblical scholar, there are a couple of items routinely mentioned and which are particularly tied to the religious culture and mind-set of the ancient Jewish people. First, the story correlates with the book of Deuteronomy. Jesus produces a successful approach to temptation where the Jewish people had historically failed. In fact, He quotes this book in his response to Satan's attempt at manipulation. Secondly, the story reveals Jesus' immovable and faithful obedience to God's will. However, there is a third aspect here, an aspect that relates to *all* of humanity: their wrestling with temptation. The point cannot be stressed enough how important it is that we remember the authentic nature of Jesus' humanness. If Jesus was never tempted, how human was He, really? If Jesus never experienced what it feels like to be approached by temptation, how human was He? If Jesus never wrestled with temptation, if He never had to make a choice in order to overcome it, how human was He? The temptation story responds to all of this. It shows that Jesus literally took upon Himself the human experience, that He wrestled, and that He won the match.

The story, found in Luke 4:1-13, reads like this:

> Jesus, full of the Holy Spirit, left the Jordan and was led by the Spirit into the wilderness, where for forty days he was tempted by the devil. He ate nothing during those days, and at the end of them he was hungry.
>
> The devil said to him, "If you are the Son of God, tell this stone to become bread."
>
> Jesus answered, "It is written: 'Man shall not live on bread alone.'"
>
> The devil led him up to a high place and showed him in an instant all the kingdoms of the world. And he said to

him, "I will give you all their authority and splendor; it has been given to me, and I can give it to anyone I want to. If you worship me, it will all be yours."

Jesus answered, "It is written: 'Worship the Lord your God and serve him only.'"

The devil led him to Jerusalem and had him stand on the highest point of the temple. "If you are the Son of God," he said, "throw yourself down from here. For it is written:

"'He will command his angels concerning you to guard you carefully; they will lift you up in their hands, so that you will not strike your foot against a stone.'"

Jesus answered, "It is said: 'Do not put the Lord your God to the test.'"

When the devil had finished all this tempting, he left him until an opportune time.

Jesus Defeats the Trinity of Human Temptation

As we can see in this story, there are three specific temptations administered by the Devil. These temptations represent those that we all face and wrestle with in some way, shape, or form. The first temptation Jesus faces is that of the physical; the kind addressed in this story refers to the physical suffering and weakness produced by hunger. However, this specific temptation embodies the encompassing temptation we encounter to fulfill our own physical desires. All human beings have physical desires (or appetites, if you will) they are tempted to satisfy. Most men, for instance, have a sexual appetite of sorts. This physical hunger seeks satisfaction, and it is often fulfilled through a promiscuous manner and therefore outside the likes of a marital or even committed relationship. Thus, men end up in a cycle of feeding their hunger and using people (women) in the process. Another physical desire that has a way into the human life is that of money. Money in and of itself is not a problem. We know this. It's when financial prosperity becomes the primary goal in one's life that it evolves into a real problem. All in all, this first temptation addresses people's temptation to feed their selfishness in the form of the physical (i.e. our earthly desires). Jesus' response to this temptation is "It is written: 'man shall not live on bread alone.'" In other words, we are more than flesh and bone. We are spiritual beings made in the image of our Creator, and our spiritual health is even more vital.

The second temptation refers to the human desire for authority and recognition. There is an innate desire within the human will to seek after praise. Remember, though, what was addressed in the second chapter of this book. *It's not about you.* And this is true for the Christian as well as the non-Christian. The difference, however, is that the Christian has entered into a state of being in which the self-praise that they are tempted to fulfill is combated with humility. This humility is built into the human spirit by God Himself. The second temptation addresses people's temptation to fulfill their selfishness in the form of self-righteousness. It relates to the human desire to essentially be as God. Jesus' response to this temptation is, "It is written: 'Worship the Lord your God and serve him only.'" Translation: there is only one God, to whom all authority and recognition belongs.

The third temptation refers to the human desire for power and glory, and the attempt to manipulate God in order to achieve it. Every person tries to develop their own plans and goals for their life. And thus there is the temptation to create our own blueprint and attempt to use God in order to achieve the goals outlined within it. The blueprint is self-created, self-influenced, and self-motivated. The objective is to make God fit into it however we see fit. The third temptation addresses humans' temptation to fulfill their selfishness in the form of control. Jesus' response to this temptation is, "It is said: 'Do not put the Lord your God to the test.'" In short, God is not a resource to be manipulated.

What we come to find in all of this is that Jesus is the very model for human living. He directly faces the challenges of the human struggle and defeats them. He wrestles with the challenges of life and with the temptations to live counter to God's intentions for His human creation. The important thing to recognize is that Jesus wrestles with these things, and overcomes them, *as a human being*. As the scriptures tell us, Jesus "who, being in very nature God, did not consider equality with God something to be used to his own advantage; rather, he made himself nothing by taking the very nature of a servant, being made in human likeness. And being found in appearance as a man, he humbled himself by becoming obedient to death—even death on a cross!" (Philippians 2:6–8). Jesus did not have an advantage. He emptied Himself of His divine qualities, and thus was as vulnerable to temptation and the difficulties of life as any other person. He approached life as a human, wrestled as a human, and conquered as a human.

What does this mean for us? Well, have you ever considered Jesus' words in John 14:12–13? He says, "Very truly I tell you, whoever believes in me will do the works I have been doing, and they will do even greater things than these, because I am going to the Father. And I will do whatever you ask in my name, so that the Father may be glorified in the Son." This statement should make you feel slightly uncomfortable and yet empowered at the same time. The discomfort lies in the truth that we are capable of wrestling with the temptations and hardships of life as successfully as Jesus did. This bears an immense expectation! It's easy to dismiss our ability to combat life's issues in the way that Jesus did because of the mere fact that He was Jesus. As suggested previously, we can get so hung up on the divine nature of Jesus that His mission and success become solely tied to His divinity. This produces thoughts of, *Well, of course He could live life in such a way. He was God.* But Jesus Himself counteracts this statement. Instead of suggesting that He is some sort of superhuman, Jesus merely states that He is obedient to the Father's will. That's it. Jesus accomplished what He did because He devoted his life and vocation to God's will. And this is why Jesus can make the statement that He does in reference to us (His followers). If we simply emulate Him in His obedience to God's will, we too can accomplish what He did, and even more! But here's the theological brain stretch ... we are able to do this not of our own effort, but through Jesus and His spirit enabling us to do so. As the Apostle Paul said, "I can do all things through Christ who gives me strength" (Philippians 4:13).

Wrestling is a Mini-Life

In this chapter, we have recognized that wrestling is a part of the human experience. And as I have tried to show (and will continue to show) throughout this book, in relation to the proposed concepts, the sport of wrestling serves as a physical imagery. Just as wrestling is a part of the human experience, so is the sport of wrestling a mini-life. It's sort of a life within a life. The ups and downs, wins and losses, mental lapses, growth and toughness, triumphs and setbacks, and yes, even temptations, all take place within a single wrestling season. Moreover, the experiences that take place within the season seem to move along a stream of time that allows no room for stagnancy. The season will continue to move along with or without you. In some respects, a wrestling season is like life at hyper-speed. There's a faster pace at play. And if you don't keep up, you'll find yourself lost, confused, and altogether left behind. This is perhaps why a lot of wrestlers end up tired by the end of the season. Arguably, it's not so much a physical fatigue. It's more an emotional and mental fatigue. Everything is happening and being experienced at such a fast pace that an individual can grow tired by the end of it all. Some wrestlers need a chance to step outside the fast stream of the wrestling mini-life and allow themselves a chance to recover, reflect, rejuvenate, and begin preparing for the next season.

One of the positive elements of this is the correlation between the fast pace of the wrestling mini-life with that of the potential fast character growth and maturity of the individual wrestler. I've mentioned already that the sport of wrestling has a unique ability to aid individuals in the building of their character. What hasn't been mentioned until now, however, is that this takes place at a quick speed. Many coaches have identified this particular element within the sport, and have, as a result, communicated to their wrestlers that part of their job as a coach is to train them to be tough, committed, accountable, and goal-oriented human beings. They are being trained for life.

Wrestling is a part of the human experience. The sport of wrestling takes this aspect, replicates it, and produces a mini-life of this experience in action.

CHAPTER 7

COMMUNITY

I n wrestling, in Christianity, in most anything relative
to human existence is the importance and necessity of
community. We were created for community. We were
designed to be in relational contact with other human beings.
We were purposed to be partially dependent on others. And
the reason for this is not simply to avoid being alone or to
intentionally remove focus off ourselves, but to essentially
better ourselves as human beings—to help one another grow
and develop in every facet of what it means to be human.

A Biblical Understanding of Community

The concept of community is absolutely essential to
understanding the God of the Christian faith and our
relationship to Him. If we are to take seriously the notion that
the God of the Bible is a triune God, then we must consider
the truth that God, in and of Himself, is community (Father,
Son, and Holy Spirit). Thus it should follow that as those
created in the image of God, we were intentionally designed
for community. Even more so, it should follow that, in the very
act of creating, God was inviting and making available the

possibility that we could one day be a part of *His* community. In other words, that we could partake in communion with Him; we could be in relationship with Him—a living, perfect community. As a matter of fact, this is, in essence, what is meant by the very notion that "God is love." C. S. Lewis wrote about this in his famous Christian apologetic piece, *Mere Christianity.*

> All sorts of people are fond of repeating the Christian statement that 'God is love'. But they seem not to notice that the words 'God is love' have no real meaning unless God contains at least two Persons. Love is something that one person has for another person. If God was a single person, then before the world was made, He was not love. Of course, what these people mean when they say that God is love is often something quite different: they really mean 'Love is God'. They really mean that our feelings of love, however and wherever they arise, and whatever results they produce, are to be treated with great respect. Perhaps they are: but that is something quite different from what Christians mean by the statement 'God is love'. They believe that the living, dynamic activity of love has been going on in God forever and has created everything else. And that, by the way, is perhaps the most important difference between Christianity and all other religions: that in Christianity God is not a static thing—not even a person—but a dynamic, pulsating activity, a life, almost a kind of drama.[8]

Do you remember in the first chapter, it was suggested that part of the gospel message is an invitation to be a part of the grand story of God—a story that He is working toward fulfilling? Within this is the concept of community highlighted above. Within this "God story" is a community (the church). And the ultimate destination for this community is God—*the*

---

[8]   C. S. Lewis, *Mere Christianity*, Signature Classics Edition (New York, NY: HarpersCollins, 2009).

community, the perfect, dynamic community that was the purpose of God enacting creation in the first place.

Community is a Gift

Community itself is a gracious gift from God, especially as it relates to Christian community. To live in Christian community is to live in the presence of God. For it is the Christian belief that God is present in the life of every follower, and that therefore to be in fellowship with other believers is to be in fellowship with God Himself (Matthew 18:20). It is a foreshadowing of the community that awaits us—the perfect community by which we will fully partake in communion with the triune God and that of our fellow believers in Christ.

"Christian community means community through Jesus Christ and in Jesus Christ" (Dietrich Bonhoeffer).[9] We belong to one another through and in (and *only* through and in) Jesus Christ. We are those who recognize that, without Christ, there is discord between God and humanity, that Christ has become the mediator of peace with God as well as peace among human beings.

Again, because we are in Christ, we are a community whose destination lies in eternity. Upon this life, we will continue as a community of grace. Therefore, in our present state, we are brought together in order to come alongside one another and train—to exercise our strength and abilities in the faith. We not only bear each other's burdens, as Christ bore the burden of all humanity, but we also challenge one another. We reject stagnancy. We reject mediocrity. A community of faith is a community that seeks the will of God—a will that is constantly attacked, but never overcome, by the will of evil. And we, as

---

[9]   Dietrich Bonhoeffer, *Life Together: The Classic Exploration of Faith in Community*, First HarperOne Edition (New York, NY: HarperOne, 2009).

advocates of God's will, are commissioned to battle against evil. We are to stand on the side of victory. We are to seek to overcome evil with good.

Wrestling Community

Virtually every wrestler has experienced the camaraderie that transpires on a team. Whether or not each individual wrestler is friends with their teammates outside of the wrestling room, they are all nevertheless friends during the season. During that time, every member is integral to the atmosphere of the team. Every member contributes something, and they all utilize one another in order to make it through moments of training and hardship, whether it's related to wrestling or something personal. They lean on one another. In many cases, they become a close-knit family. What one wrestler is going through, they all go through together.

To take this even beyond the context of one's own team, it is absolutely vital for the wrestling community as a whole to work together. The more we work together, the more we push each other, the more the sport itself develops competitively. Because as long as new things within the sport are discovered and shared, the more it becomes required for even newer styles, moves, tactics, ideas to be sought after, which pushes the sport in directions it couldn't have otherwise gone before. Part of the beauty of wrestling is that there is no end. There will always remain trails to be blazed, new things that cause the sport to become more and more competitive, requiring wrestlers themselves to work even harder to achieve success. For the idea is not to simply be successful as a competitor. It's about serving as one who helps grow the sport, as one who becomes a part of the force that thrusts it into new and exciting directions.

The Ohio Wrestler

Several years ago, I was reading some articles following the conclusion of another NCAA Division I tournament. In the course of my reading, I came across a story that has stuck with me ever since. A wrestler from Ohio State University, Jeff, was being interviewed following his national championship. He gave his thoughts regarding the season: the ups, the downs, and of course his elated experience as a national champion. However, as the interview progressed, Jeff revealed an individual who was integral to his success behind the scenes. This individual, named TJ, was a fellow teammate and fifth-year senior. Just like any guy who has put in his time as a Division I wrestler, TJ was seeking after a national championship and had just one year of eligibility left in order to do so. He had qualified for the national tournament two previous years, and both times came up empty handed. Nevertheless, as the season approached, he found that he was in the same weight class as his friend, Jeff, a returning All-American. He began to think about his wrestling career, how he had been plagued with injuries, and how he had yet to accomplish what he had set out to do. He thought about what his purpose in the sport was. And then it dawned on him: perhaps wrestling is not about him. The result of this thought process brought about the most unorthodox approach to achieving a national championship I had ever heard. TJ was going to win a national championship, but it wasn't going to be him, necessarily, who assumed the title. TJ was going to *make* a national champion.

When the head coach approached him about having a wrestle-off for the starting position, TJ simply responded, "There can only be one national champion at 141 pounds, and there's already one in the line-up." He told the coaches he was willing to sacrifice everything as if he were wrestling to make sure Jeff won the title. And he did. As Jeff reflected on TJ's commitment during the interview, he said, "He was my roommate and my best friend. We trained together, worked out together—we did everything the same. He was eating the right way, going to bed early, and helped me keep my head in there until it was done."

Jeff had obstacles of his own to overcome, including an injury that occurred in the championship match in order to win the title. However, none of that meant as much to Jeff as what TJ did for him. "Outside of the coaches and my dad, he has been the most influential person in my success. That is one of the most selfless things I have ever watched someone do in wrestling or seen in my everyday life. To be the person getting his hand raised makes me appreciate what TJ did even more."

This story is a beautiful example of wrestling community, as well as a beautiful expression of humility. The reason why community and humility are so part and parcel to one another is because genuine community *requires* humility. It takes a very selfless person to do what the Ohio wrester, TJ, did. In order for him to enact this whole situation, he had to sacrifice his own dreams and be willing to take partial ownership of his friend's dreams and goals instead. The coaches, TJ, and Jeff all had to do their part in order to make the goal a reality.

CHAPTER 8

DISCIPLESHIP

The purpose of the Christian faith is discipleship (Matthew 28:18-20). And discipleship requires an imitation and movement toward whom you are following. It demands (as has been continuously suggested in this book) a withdrawal from personal authority and a surrendering of that authority to the one who is discipling you. As Christians, we have submitted our own authority and exchanged it for God's authority in our lives. A disciple does as Christ does, moves as Christ moves, speaks as Christ speaks. A disciple of Christ seeks to emulate Him. The goal is not personal recognition, but for God to be revealed in the act of discipleship. All in all, works—those things which transpire as a result of our discipleship—are not put into action for means of personal moral gain, but for the sole means of revealing God in the process. In other words, we, as disciples of Christ, desire for Him to be revealed in a very real way to others. We permit Him to move through us, act through us, speak through us, so that He is identified. And it's not the case that God can't or doesn't reveal Himself by other means. He does. However, it is yet another gracious gift from God for His disciples—a gift in allowing us to play a part in expressing His glory to the world, both individually and as a community.

The important thing here is that genuine Christian faith comes with a cost: the cost of discipleship. It's a cost that calls everything to the table. Who you are as a human being is brought before the Lord and sacrificed in exchange for something far greater: God Himself through the power of Christ and the Holy Spirit. You assume a new identity in Christ.

Disciples Head in a New Direction with a New Leader

In the second century, and only a hundred or so years after the death and resurrection of Jesus, there lived a highly influential Christian apologist named Irenaeus. One of his most profound interpretations in Christian theology is termed the recapitulation theory. This is essentially a fancy title corresponding to his idea explaining the incarnation of Christ and our relationship to Him as His followers (His disciples). It basically says this: ancient Adam used to be the head (or leader) of the human race. Humanity was therefore traveling in the direction of disobedience. But then Jesus stepped in. Jesus became the new Adam and *recapitulated* the experience of the first Adam, leading the human race from a life of *disobedience* to God into a life of *obedience*. He thus became the new leader of the human race. To be a follower of Christ, to be His disciple, was to follow His lead. Of course there is much more depth to this theory, but this is the gist of it, and it seems to provide a relatively good picture of what it looks like to be a Christian disciple.

Discipleship in Wrestling

One is not called into wrestling as a spectator or one who simply experiences the sport. To be a wrestler, you must surrender your will, and in so doing, engage the direction and teaching of those who have the power to influence you positively in the sport. In a sense, you become a disciple of those whose experience, technique, and abilities exceed your own. You allow their expertise to mold and shape you into a skilled and driven wrestler.

Once you've reached a certain level of maturity in the sport, where you have developed into a relative expert yourself, you then surround yourself with other serious competitors in order to push not only yourself but them as well. When true competitors seek out one another, the results can only move in a positive direction. This means not just seeking out each other in tournament settings, but actually training with one another, actually forcing yourself to be put in a situation where you're learning and adapting to what skills and abilities others offer. When this happens, it forces wrestlers to seek out new technique, skills, ideas, and methods to utilize in order to win a match. It causes the sport to grow and mature; and it causes each wrestler to grow and mature as well.

Buzz

One of the greatest men I have ever met was a man who would probably be considered average in terms of accolades and success. I met him when I ventured out to the desert of Bakersfield, California, to wrestle for Cal State. His name was Brian Busby. We called him Buzz. He didn't look like a wrestler, nor did he wrestle like a typical wrestler. He had an unorthodox style but was very aggressive and unbelievably strong.

Buzz was the hardest worker in the wrestling room. And his Christian faith was absolutely inspiring. This man would tackle the classroom with tenacity, expend amazing effort during wrestling practice, put in an extra workout after practice, and still find time to prepare a message for each week's Bible study. We had a wrestling Bible study once a week at Buzz's house. We would sing songs together, pray together, and then Buzz would deliver his message. One would think that a man of this sort of dedication would exude a personality of remarkable confidence. But he didn't. Buzz was humble. He was always self-reflective, aware of his limitations and failures, and put others before himself.

Buzz broke the line-up as a senior. Though his record was average, his effort was far from it. You could always count on him to put forth his best. And he loved it. He loved to wrestle! At a time in my life when the work as a college wrestler didn't seem worth it, Buzz's perseverance confused me. I simply didn't understand it. He was only winning matches half of the time, which means that the other half of the time, he was on the losing end. This didn't seem enjoyable. Nevertheless, he loved wrestling. He loved the fight. He loved the training. He loved the warrior mentality. Buzz, though frustrated with losses, had a much more mature understanding of wrestling. He was a true disciple of the sport.

Perhaps the most amazing thing about Buzz was that he became a leader. We had a returning All-American on the team and another wrestler who would become an All-American that year, but Buzz was considered by most to be the leader. He was not only outspoken in his words, he was outspoken in his life. He led by example. And we listened. We all respected him.

Just like any other wrestler, Buzz wanted to be the best. And he went after it. He dedicated hours, days, and years of his life to striving after wrestling success. And even though he failed to achieve his goals by the end of his career, it didn't matter all that much. He enjoyed the journey, and he grew into a highly respected leader in the process, someone I wish I could emulate. Few people have impacted my life in the way that Buzz did. The interesting thing is that Buzz and I weren't the best of friends, per se. We were certainly friends, but his impact on my life came not from our friendship. It came from merely watching him live his life with power and conviction.

The Tough Road

Being a disciple of something does not promise success. Being a disciple of something means becoming a follower and advocate of it with the understanding that the journey might be riddled with pain, difficulty or even failure. It's a tough road. But you believe in it wholeheartedly. You believe that it contains immeasurable value with respect to your life. You believe that, without it, you are a different person. Buzz clearly understood the nature of discipleship, as it corresponds to both wrestling and the Christian faith.

CHAPTER 9

THE FREEDOM TO BE

O ne of the overarching themes within this book is the notion of surrendering the will in exchange for partnership in the will of God. The rhetoric can seem rather passive. In fact, the concept of sin, and our common understanding of it, can also often cause us to perceive a passive approach. Thus far, I have suggested that a surrendering of the will in exchange for obedience to God's is freeing. But what is actually meant by that? In what way is it freeing?

If we are to understand sin more clearly, it is imperative that we shine a light upon two aspects of it. The first aspect is freedom from the bondage or slavery of sin. The second is the freedom *to*—the freedom to live as God intended, the freedom to realize our potential. Simply put, the relationship of freedom to sin is a freedom *from* as well as a freedom *to*. When we engage in a relationship with Christ, we are freed *from* the bondage of sin, and freed *to go and live*, leaving the chains of sin behind us. If we are going to talk about one aspect of freedom, we must talk about the other as well. The truth of this is highlighted in Jesus' own words upon forgiving people of their sins, "go and sin no more" (John 8:11), "go in peace" (Luke 7:50), etc.

In the opening chapter, I introduced an alternative, technical understanding of sin as a "missing of an opportunity," an opportunity to be a part of God's story. I also suggested that what we obtain in the course of responding positively to this opportunity is our true self. We are given freedom to be a part of God's unfolding story, and freedom to be the person God intended for us to be. We are given the freedom to approach the world with more power and conviction than we ever had the opportunity to do before.

So as you can see, there is an individual element at play here. One of the ideas brought forth through the Renaissance, and into the Reformation, was a more individualistic component to the faith. Prior to the birth of full-fledged individualism, the way in which human beings approached the faith was primarily through a communal mind-set. In other words, a human being was simply a piece of the whole. The role of the individual was to help and contribute to the function and well-being of the larger community. What individualism did was, in part, empower the dignity of the individual human being. The individual was, in some respects, a freethinking master of his or her own. This has proven to be both a curse and a blessing. The curse is that we quickly ran with individualistic thought and lost sight of much of the importance of community. The blessing is that acquiring a sense of individualism has allowed us to identify the innate power available within each of us serving in the kingdom of God. The hope is that we can develop a balance between individualism and community. But given the fact that we are prone to individualistic thought, it's at least helpful to allow the fruit of that thinking to produce proactive and faithful people.

The Power of the Individual Wrestler

One of the supremely unique elements of the sport of wrestling pertains to its individualism. A wrestler has the ability to chase after and achieve championships all on their own, with no requirement needed by teammates to get the job done. In sports that are more team oriented, you could very well sit on the sidelines or bench and contribute absolutely nothing, and yet when it's all said and done, still be permitted the honor and title of national or world champion. This doesn't really happen in wrestling. If you want to be a champion, being passive isn't going to get you anywhere. If you want to be a champion, you have to go after it. Mirroring the concept we highlighted in the beginning of this chapter, the freedom you acquire as an individual wrestler is twofold. You have the skills and talent. But you also have the freedom to put them to use, to pursue your potential. You have to go. You have to wrestle.

Jayson Ness

When Jayson was a young boy, he wrote a letter to Jay Robinson, the head wrestling coach at the University of Minnesota. This letter said that he was going to wrestle and coach at the University of Minnesota someday. Jayson started wrestling as a six-year-old, when he found a wrestling flier and brought it home to his parents. He initially thought that it was for professional wrestling: a chance to muscle up, jump off the ropes, and body slam his opponents. And even though the wrestling world he stepped into was very different than the one he had in mind, he nevertheless fell in love with the sport.

After his first year proved to be rather difficult—he only won a single match—the following years were filled with success. Upon achieving many city and state championships as a kid, he went on to win two state titles in Minnesota at the high school level. While Jayson entertained interest in other colleges, when the time for choosing a school came around, he remembered the letter he wrote as a young wrestler and knew that he wanted to compete for the University of Minnesota.

Jayson's faith was something of a private venture for him. His family wasn't much involved in the church, though he still managed to go through confirmation in the Lutheran church at some point in his childhood. There was an element of faith for sure. But his faith was still in infancy as he entered his freshman year in college. During the first wrestling meeting with the team, a guy named Tom was invited in for a short presentation. Tom was a member of AIA (Athletes in Action). He was a former wrestler himself. He talked about his faith and the opportunity for each of the wrestlers to individually meet with him and explore their faith. The notion caught Jayson's attention, and he signed up. These individual meetings with Tom throughout his college years—reading the Bible, praying, and working through his faith—changed his life forever.

Jayson experienced tremendous success as a Division I college wrestler. He achieved All-American honors as a freshman, placing fifth in the NCAA tournament. By his sophomore year, he was already competing for a national title. He faced a strong opponent from Indiana in the NCAA finals, and he came up short. The loss hurt, but rather than burying himself in sorrow, Jayson had this crazy notion that perhaps losing in the national finals wasn't the end of the world. Perhaps God had something else planned. In fact, this loss seemed to be another turning point for him. Heading into his junior year, Jayson decided it was time to take his walk with Christ even more seriously. He stepped away from the party scene, which was filled with drinking binges, and instead decided that he was going to immerse himself in reading the Bible, growing in his faith, and building stronger relationships. Relationships had always been a central component to his love for the sport of wrestling. For him, the friendships, the camaraderie discovered on a wrestling team were worth far more than gold medals.

Jayson went up a weight class. The adjustment was difficult. By the end of the season, and heading into the national tournament, he had lost more matches in that single season than he had in both his freshman and sophomore years combined. Nevertheless, Tom helped him focus on his faith as well as on competing to his potential. Jayson's unwavering focus had him barely missing the NCAA finals again, and finishing as an All-American for the third straight season—a third-place finish.

By his senior year, his faith had become so much a part of him that he couldn't help but talk about it. Every interview after his wrestling matches was an opportunity to take the eyes of spectators off of him and onto God. He was undefeated throughout the entire season, and worked his way back to the finals of the NCAA tournament. His opponent was a familiar one: an Iowa wrestler whom he had defeated handily a couple weeks prior at the Big Ten tournament. However, the match started off as a repeat of two years ago, when he had lost on the big stage. As the time on the clock began to slip away, Jayson began to see his national championship dreams slip away along with it. Only seconds remained in the match, and he needed a takedown just to tie the match and send it into overtime. Jayson said a quick prayer in his head for the Lord to give him strength to finish the match, and immediately attacked his opponent with everything he had. Each attempt he made to take his opponent down, though it failed, drew him closer and closer, until Jayson finally ducked underneath him, wrapped his arms around his waist, and drove his opponent to the mat. Jayson not only earned the takedown but persisted to hold him on his back, earning back points and an extraordinary finish and win! Jayson Ness won a national championship in the last seconds of his wrestling career!

When Jayson was interviewed after the match, his focus never shifted. It was still all about God, not about Jayson. The glory was God's; Jayson simply enjoyed basking in its presence. You see, Jayson experienced a sense of freedom in the course of his college wrestling career—freedom to be the best person and the best wrestler he could be. But in order to do any of this upon choosing to follow Jesus, he had to live and he had to compete. And this is the primary objective: to wholeheartedly compete. No matter the outcome, the human objective is to be a competitor, a true competitor. If the outcome results in your favor, great; it's a wonderful thing to experience victory. If the outcome does not result in your favor ... so what; though the outcome is defeating, your life and its purpose have not been defeated. Losing hurts. Losing is far from desirable. Losing weighs heavy on the heart. But your objective is to compete in order to express God's glory in your life.

CHAPTER **10**

LIFE

I f you've ever truly thought about it, life is short. The time allotted to take advantage of all that life has to offer is minimal and seems to escape us. There's a window of opportunity to pursue elusive hopes and dreams, and there will certainly come a time in which the window closes. And when that time comes, when we are past the window and looking back, we will find ourselves in one of three categories: (1) we were on the side of great achievement, (2) we tried but failed, or (3) we never even allowed ourselves to be a part of the pursuit. We deemed certain hopes and dreams to be unattainable or perhaps unrealistic, and thus decided to remove ourselves from the playing field.

Within the sport of wrestling (and certainly within most any sport), the ability to chase after great achievement is extremely short. In the midst of all that's been said within this book, I want to make it clear that the desire for greatness, the pursuit of success, is all well and good. It only becomes an issue when we've lost sight of God's agenda for our life and replaced it with our own. In other words, the desire and pursuit to be a champion, perhaps even the greatest champion that ever stepped foot on the mat, is laudable, even encouraged.

But the question is: who is it for? Moreover, are you trying to build yourself up in reaction to issues, personal issues of self-esteem or self-worth that have nothing to do with wrestling? Is it a campaign for your own honor and praise? Or is it a campaign of worship, of putting into action and trying to faithfully expend a gift, a talent, that God has given you?

You see, it's not so much about the desire or pursuit as it stands. It's about the heart of the matter. What is driving it? Remember in a previous chapter the brief discussion of *icon* versus *idol*? An icon, in short, is that which serves as a pointer to God, while an idol is something which serves as a replacement for Him. We, as human beings were designed to be icons. In fact, the word used to express that we are "made in the image of God" is *eikon* (icon) in the Greek translation. Our being a new creation in Christ is a process in which God is, by His Spirit, recreating us into fully-fledged, living and breathing *eikons*. We are, therefore, meant to be beings who point to God—His glory, His honor, and His ultimate plan for His creation. When we are not living as *eikons*, we are not living within the divine-intended purpose of our humanness. We are, instead, living in contrast to this purpose, and thus *working against* this purpose and the plan of restoration that was made known in Christ and will be consummated in His return. Quite simply, the age-old saying, "If you're not for me, you're against me," bears a great deal of truth in this respect. If you are not living as an *eikon*, you are not serving as one aligned with the redemptive purposes of God. By default, and because there is no middle ground (God's restored new creation *will be* fulfilled. The truth of this is embodied in the person of Christ: in His life, death and resurrection) you are serving as a created being that is not following the path on which God is carrying His creation. You are heading in the opposite direction altogether.

Wrestling is a Gift

Again, if God has blessed you in the sport of wrestling, and if wrestling is something in which you find a sense of joy and relative fulfillment, by all means, it is God's desire for you to put into action this blessing. Wrestling is a gift. And when it comes to a gift, the giver desires for the person receiving it to take satisfaction and delight in it. He or she is not looking for a brief confirmation of pleasure, but for one to literally take hold of what is being offered and seek to utilize whatever it may be to its fullest potential. So if you've developed some notion within this reading that God's desire for you is to take a careless approach to the sport, you've missed the big picture completely! A divine gift is a purposeful gift. It's a gift that is given by God, and He takes pleasure in seeing His recipients seek to expend it. It has Him smiling when it is received and employed with gratitude.

Might there be wrestling in God's restored creation (i.e. heaven)? Perhaps. But if it's the case that it's not (and even if it is, rather), I suggest seeking after membership in the first category (i.e. the side of great achievement). This would at the very least, depending on the outcome, place you in the second category (i.e. tried but failed). And the second category shouldn't be one that produces fear. Failure should not be feared. Most mature competitors would (I'm quite certain) affirm that failure has the potential to produce knowledge and strength. For one thing, failure suggests that you actually put forth the effort to achieve something. You took the risk and went for it. And it's this sort of attitude and resolute character that God is pleased with, and that He desires in His people toward matters of life *and* faith.

When Heaven Meets Earth

In order to grasp a genuine understanding of the above, it's essential to bear in mind a more accurate understanding of heaven and earth, of the spiritual and physical. Unfortunately, the Western world has inherited a belief of dualism, in which heaven and earth are comprised of two separate realms. Apart from the miraculous, heaven and earth keep to themselves, hence the thriving notion within many Christian circles of going to heaven when we die. While there remains an element of truth to such an idea, this is not an accurate reflection of Christianity but instead a product of Western philosophy interwoven within Christianity. This philosophy has created a Christianity in which heaven and earth do not intersect. The truth of the matter is that, within the Christian faith, heaven and earth *do* intersect. They are not two mutually exclusive realms of being, but two realms that overlap, with the heavenly realm slowly but surely taking over the earthly. In other words, at the beginning of creation was a reality in which heaven and earth perfectly coalesced. Since the Fall, however, this coalescing began to diminish and separate, pulling the two realms farther and farther away from each other. But the incarnation of Christ interrupted this. The incarnation was not merely the incarnation of God with humanity. It was the pure and unparalleled intersection of heaven and earth, and the reversal of the direction in which creation was headed. The incarnation was the point at which heaven and earth reunited and began the process of closing the gap between the two.

So when we talk about such things on earth having an effect on heaven (the physical impacting the spiritual, and vice versa), it is because the two realms are connected. In fact, the Lord's prayer—the supplication of Christ—only makes sense with this understanding in mind (i.e. "on earth as it is in heaven"). Where am I going with this? Well, in short, part of bringing heaven to earth is putting into action the blessings God has provided. When a wrestler competes, and does so as an act of worship, expending everything they have in pursuit of victory, heaven meets earth. No matter the outcome, heaven has met earth. Moreover, when heaven meets earth, it is a glimpse into the kingdom of God. For the kingdom of God (or kingdom of heaven) is not just heaven itself, but His reign. It is a description of the authority and governance He has over His creation: an authority and governance that will fully break into the world upon the return of Christ.

And ultimately, this is our duty: to advocate for the reign of God. Christians are those who have acknowledged that the reign of God has broken into the world, and that it is working toward consuming it. And yes, we do this in our wrestling and other areas in life, because, again, it's the heart of the matter. It's the intentionality of it all.

Here's a brief lesson concerning the teachings of Jesus found in the Gospels. When asked what the greatest commandment of the Law was, Jesus responded, "Love the Lord your God with all your heart and with all your soul and with all your mind. This is the first and greatest commandment. And the second is like it: 'Love your neighbor as yourself.' All the Law and the Prophets hang on these two commandments" (Matthew 22:37–40). Essentially, Jesus summed up the entire Law, all 613 commandments, into the heart of the matter. If your intention is aligned with love (that of God and others), the entire Law is fulfilled. Jesus stated, "It's all about the intentionality. It's all about the heart." If this is aligned properly, then your life as a person of God is reflective of His divine purposes, both for *your* life and for His creation as a whole.

CHAPTER 11

HOPE, MEANING, AND PURPOSE

W ith the previous chapter remaining in the backdrop, the concept of life bears even more immediate relevance with respect to its relationship to wrestling. I have mentioned quite consistently the notion of hope, meaning, and purpose in life. Though up to this point, I have written about it in rather vague terms. My goal in this particular chapter is to provide a clearer understanding of what I'm talking about with respect to these concepts.

Wrestling and Life

Without hope, meaning, and purpose, wrestling is altogether meaningless. But the truth is that wrestlers do not wrestle for nothing. And this is another way in which the role of a wrestler mirrors the Christian life. Simply wrestling, with no goals in mind, is just not an accurate description of wrestlers themselves. A wrestler is working toward something, toward victory: first, in relation to the single match, and second, in relation to etching closer to achieving a championship title of some sort. Or the wrestler is working toward expending their efforts; putting forth their best in order to utilize and express a gift, a talent, and a blessing that God has provided them (as we have discussed already). There is intention behind the wrestling that ensues. The same is true for the Christian life. The Christian life itself is one that embodies intention: of hope, meaning, and purpose. In fact, when a person engages the faith, this is exactly what the spirit of God brings. To believe in the Christian faith is to obtain *hope* that there is more to life than the here and now, and that the world will one day be redeemed, evidenced through the life, death, and resurrection of Jesus. It's to believe that the present life has *meaning*; we are God's special creation and a part of His grand story. And it's to believe that life is filled with *purpose*: how I live my life and treat others matters and has everlasting consequences.

Now, in a secular, atheistic worldview, we are encouraged to believe that meaning and purpose are products of the power within each individual. Life itself holds a purely existential component relative to meaning and purpose. In other words, life is what you make it. As the famous French, existentialist philosopher Jean-Paul Sartre stated,

> Man simply is. Not that he is simply what he conceives himself to be, but he is what he wills, and as he conceives himself after already existing – as he wills to be after that leap towards existence. Man is nothing else but that which he makes of himself.[10]

The downside, of course, is that this is it. There is essentially nothing beyond it. You live and you die. How you carry yourself and treat others is only important in so far as it affects your own personal comfort and happiness. Furthermore, hope is irrelevant apart from the potential for a more civilized society

---

[10] Jean-Paul Sartre, "Existentialism is a Humanism", lecture given in 1946. Translator Philip Mairet.

once you are gone from this world (of which this hope has no bearing on your life, as your life is no more, and there is no life beyond the present). So what you find in this worldview is nothing more than narcissism. However, what God brings (the Christian God, in particular) is something far better than some uninspiring notion of man-made meaning and purpose mixed with missing hope. God Himself brings hope, meaning, and purpose; and the face of Jesus is our most powerful sign.

Time

Both wrestling and life encompass every facet of time relative to human existence: the past, present, and future. The wrestler, with every moment, is living in the past, present, and future. The Christian, with every moment, is living in the past, present, and future. Allow me to give you an example of what I am talking about here. When a wrestler encounters his opponent, his mind and body are, in a sense, working through all these facets at once. During a match, each interaction— attempts to attack or counter, shots for a takedown or defending oncoming shots—are being met with decisions and actions. "I tried this move. It didn't work. When I made this adjustment, I got the angle I wanted, but didn't take advantage of the opening." The past is informing the present, and the present outcome is informing the future. Will they get the takedown? Will they win the match? Will they get what they hope for?

When it comes to God and the Christian life, the same is true. Once an individual engages God, he or she immediately becomes a part of a cosmic family that pervades the corridors of time. The way in which the Christian lives their life becomes an interaction between the past and present, the outcome informing their future. And the future is believed to be awaiting them with a hope that promises a renewed creation and an existence of eternity with God.

Signposts of Hope

We, as Christians, are bearers of hope. We are those who have committed ourselves not only to God, but to that which God promises. And He promises a full return to His creation that carries with it renewal and a kingdom of peace. He promises an overthrow of evil and all the damage that it has done. So when we direct creation's eyes to the Creator, it's a reminder of the promise that awaits us. We are therefore signposts that lead to Him and all that He offers. And thus, when a Christian wrestler uses their platform to express this, they are not simply redirecting eyes to God but they are also serving as a signpost to the hope that awaits all creation. As we mentioned in a previous chapter, the wrestler is serving as a model of the new creation, the story that God is at work in unfolding.

Chapter 12

The Difference

Among all the similarities between wrestling and faith, there are differences as well, and there is one primary difference to note. The primary difference is this: wrestling is a means to an end, while faith is something that continues throughout a lifetime and is perfected upon the completion of this life. This is not to say former wrestlers cease to be a part of the wrestling community. Instead, it means that our life (our time) as competitors ceases to be. Put simply, we no longer put ourselves through the type of training involved with wrestling competitively. We may become coaches, whether paid or volunteer, but the training involves others. We may even *participate* in the training of our wrestlers, but it is not for our benefit but for the benefit of the wrestler who *is* in fact expending the effort toward specific goals. Our responsibility is then to deliver our knowledge and experience.

When an individual has finished their time as a wrestler, there are moments when they wish they could go back. They wish they could enter back into that time of training and competing. The problem is that, at some point, they can't. Situations in life prevent that from happening, not to mention the fact that their body won't allow it. Our physical body steeps into decline. Never again will we be in the sort of shape required to compete in the sport. Until, of course, when science and technology discover the capacity for time travel; though I wouldn't hold your breath.

With the Christian faith, the training never expires. We are called to exercise ourselves in the faith on a continuous basis. And while there are moments of rest, the rest is limited; for to remain in a state of prolonged rest will result in eventual downfall. We must remain on our guard, forever preparing ourselves for the attacks of the Evil One. Because, quite simply, the Evil One never rests; he is always on the attack. We are never to fall into the belief that our training has an expiration date. As long as we are living, we are training. And the understanding that the Evil One is always on the attack should not allow us to be complacent in remaining on the defense. Our training is not simply necessary as a means to defend ourselves in matters of the soul, but to push us toward the desire and ability to be on the *offense*. We are not merely those who live a life picking up messes, but those who pursue spiritual ground in the name of Christ. We are those who take steps forward in order to push the Evil One steps backward. Instead of constantly having our backs against the wall, we march forward, pushing the Evil One in a position where he finds himself with his own back against the wall. This shouldn't be something new or necessarily profound, either. For example, a wrestler doesn't step on the mat with a mind-set of defense. They step on the mat with the mind-set of being offensive. The idea is to attack, to score as many points as possible. The idea is to make your opponent adapt to *your* style, to wear them down, to dominate.

The problem is that most Christians don't see their faith in this way. They see it solely as a means to fill a potential emptiness or to aid them in becoming a good or better person. However, this mind-set places the Christian in a situation where they are not truly responding to the call of discipleship. They are not pursuing what God has for them. A disciple of

Christ has recognized God's call as not only a surrendering of the self, but a call into battle. They have recognized it as a call into life as a spiritual warrior of sorts. God isn't as concerned with those who decide to stand, immovable, behind the lines of battle. He's concerned with those who are willing to step forward (with His constant help) in pursuit of enemy lines. He's more concerned with those who are inspired to chase victory.

Are we victory chasers? Are we followers of a dangerous call? It's not dangerous in the sense that the outcome is defeating. We know that it's not. We know that, in the end, God wins. Instead, it's a call that's dangerous in the sense that we commit ourselves to a life that defies complacency, a life that pulls us in uncertain directions, directions that cause us to rely not on ourselves but on God alone. It means responding to a call that demands our attention, our heart, and our life.

Use wrestling as a physical mirroring. Use it as a means to, in a symbolic sense, physically experience the wrestling we face in the life of faith. Use the competitive mind-set necessary to be successful in the sport as a tool in which to approach spiritual issues and battles. And always, always, use it as a platform for Christ. Use it as a means to direct the eyes of others to the Creator.

CHAPTER 13

WHAT WE LEARNED IN 2013

In February of 2013, it was announced by the International Olympic Committee that wrestling would be put on the chopping block for the 2020 Olympic Games. The decision came as a shock to the wrestling community—and rightly so. No one ever imagined that such a decision was possible for a sport that is known as one of the original and oldest events on the Olympic slate. As a Christian, the news hit me in a different way. When wrestling was threatened with removal from the Olympic Games, I was in the midst of writing this book. One of the very premises of this work suggests that the sport of wrestling is altogether unique and inimitable in its relationship to human life and spirituality. In short, I felt that if wrestling was unable to earn its way back in, we would be losing more than just the opportunity for wrestlers to compete on the biggest and greatest athletic stage on earth; we were losing an insightful picture into the Christian life.

The first chapter in this book highlighted a very significant story in God's epic novel: Jacob wrestling with God. Though the chapter was relatively short, covering topics of interest in a sweeping fashion, hopefully readers acquired a deeper appreciation for the act of wrestling itself. Wrestling *is* the Christian faith. Whether realistically or metaphorically, every Christian is a wrestler; every human being is a wrestler. Some are winning; some are losing. Some are in the midst of war. Every human being wrestles with life and wrestles with God. And this is why the Jacob story, when looked at more closely, resonates (or should resonate) so well with us. Life is a battlefield. There are moments of peace and joy, but life is unfortunately a battlefield. If you can't seem to grasp this based on your own experience, all it takes is a simple recognition of world events on a daily basis. There are wars, rumors of wars, people being killed by the masses, children starving, power in the hands of the corrupt, and so many moral failings that one couldn't possibly keep track of them.

I have heard it time and again: "Wrestlers make the best Christians." This comment is made by wrestlers and non-wrestlers alike. This is not an empirical fact, nor something to be proven, but merely recognition by others who have noticed something unique about followers of Christ who were once competitors in the sport of wrestling. Wrestlers have lived a life of structure, training, competition, and hard-nosed devotion. Once their life in the sport has expired, they take all those characteristics that were necessary for their life as a wrestler and transfer them to their faith.

The role of the wrestler relative to the Christian life keeps the warrior mentality in the faith alive. We are sinners saved by grace. We are advocates of God's love and justice. But we are also warriors in pursuit of God's kingdom. In the beginning God created the heavens and the earth, and it was good. But human sin, coupled with the evil of Satan and his counterparts, corrupted God's good creation. Through the life, death, and resurrection of Jesus, sin and evil have been vanquished. Because of Christ, sin and evil are now heading down a course in which their only destination is a dead end. And this dead end bears their permanent destruction. Because of Christ, the kingdom of God has broken into the world. And it is slowly but surely taking it over, until the second coming of our Lord Jesus, when sin and evil will be no more. All that will remain is a world of peace and tranquility, filled with people who chose to call on His name during their time in a fallen world.

The act of wrestling doesn't only depict the human struggle against pain and evil, either. It depicts the inner struggle as well. Our relational separation from God has manifested desires that can only be fulfilled through union with Him. These desires include the longing to be loved and the need to be validated by our peers that we are good (morally and/or athletically) and that we are people of utmost importance. We all want to be somebody—somebody honored and praised, somebody who will be remembered by the world when our life is over. Before this relational separation, humanity was in perfect relationship with God, and these desires did not exist. They did not exist because all we ever needed was satisfied through relationship with Him. These desires are products of something broken, of something missing within our heart and soul. They're meant to lead us toward the only source that can sufficiently and completely fulfill them: God. When a wrestler pursues wrestling glory for their own sake, they are caught up in the game of brokenness—the meaningless cycle of self-fulfillment where accomplishments provide temporary satisfaction. Simply put, when a wrestler seeks after their own glory, the satisfaction is fleeting. But when a wrestler seeks after *God's* glory, they are afforded the opportunity to bask in *God's* glory. And this satisfaction is lasting. It's a glimpse into the glory that we will get to experience fully in eternity when we are finally and perfectly united in relationship with our Creator. Therefore, the Christian wrestler seeks after wrestling glory not for their own sake but in order to experience moments in which they can bask in the glory of God. For when the creature accomplishes a task for *His* name's sake, the creature is living as divinely intended. When the wrestler achieves champion status with the intent of making their God proud of the athlete He has created, the wrestler is wrestling as divinely intended.

In September of 2013, wrestling was voted back into the Olympics. It was a vote that carried a prevailing statement and a realization of what we learned—we need wrestling; the world needs wrestling.

Conclusion

I t wasn't until a few years ago that I realized what the sport of wrestling had done for me or its impact on my faith. Truth be told, none of what has been discussed in this book was apparent in my life. Instead of serving as an example of the fruitful information within these pages, I grew to hate the sport. In a lot of ways, I used wrestling as a measuring stick, the same way in which Nate Toedter used it, as mentioned in his story.

I entered the sport as a six-year-old, and to this day, I can still remember walking into that dim and humid room for my first practice. I experienced success pretty much from the beginning. I, for some reason or another, didn't have a growing stage like a good many young wrestlers do. From ages six to fifteen, I earned six state titles and three national titles. I entered high school in the state of Missouri as a wrestling prodigy of sorts, winning the state title as a freshman and with expectations by many to become the next four-timer. (At that time, the list of four-time state champions had only a handful of people on it.) When my family moved to Minnesota after my first year in high school—due partly because of a job transfer for my dad but mostly for reasons pertaining to personal family issues—I saw my success in terms of championships suffer. I still found winning to be a natural outcome, but I seemed to fall under pressure and lose when it counted to win. I finished in third place at the state tournament as a sophomore and junior in Minnesota, until finally climbing my way back to the top of the podium as a senior.

I wasn't highly recruited out of high school. At the time, I didn't much care. All I needed was a school to go to that would force me to leave the frozen tundra of Minnesota. Toward the end of my senior year, just a few weeks before the state tournament, my father's demons followed him, and my family fell apart. My immediate solution to this was to run away and do life on my own for a while. I received a small scholarship to attend California State University, Bakersfield. I packed my bags and took the long flight to a school I had never before visited.

My adjustment to Division I level wrestling was rough. Injuries plagued me, my self-confidence as a wrestler decreased, and my hate for the sport heightened. Needless to say, I quickly realized that running away from my problems wasn't the wisest decision, and wrestling wasn't going to help me, either. I returned to Minnesota after just a year, and my wrestling career ended.

After wrestling since childhood, and having the identity of a wrestler become so much a part of me, I was a bit lost in the process of moving forward. I approached several different courses in life before many years later deciding to pursue a degree in theology at Bethel University. My Christian faith had always been integral to my life, and the study of theology seemed to assume my primary interest and devotion where wrestling had once resided. It was around that time, however, that wrestling was revived in me: not as a competitor, but as a spectator. I started engaging in the sport again, more particularly through my following of college and international wrestling. And with the mix of the sport of wrestling and theology constantly occupying my thoughts, the premise of this book came into existence: the role of a wrestler mirrors the Christian life.

As the concept raced through my head, and as I started noticing many wrestlers choosing to be outspoken in regard to their Christian faith, I yearned to compete again. With the understandings included in this book, I knew I could enjoy the sport. I knew that I would love it! But it was too late. College eligibility for me was long past expired, and I had to work and provide for a family. Nevertheless, and though I failed to see it during my years as a competitor, wrestling taught me so much about life and about faith. I wish I could go back and do it all over again. Nonetheless, I am who I am today as a result of my years as a wrestler and as a follower of Jesus, and I am eternally grateful!

ABOUT THE AUTHOR

Michael Fessler is an author and former wrestler, competing for sixteen years. His journey into faith started around the same time he first stepped foot on the mat as a six year old. After stepping away from wrestling competitively, Michael engrossed himself in the world of theology and began to see his faith in a whole new light. To him, every Christian is a "wrestler"; and wrestling itself contains a unique perspective in regard to the Christian faith. He holds a B.A. in Biblical and Theological Studies from Bethel University and an M.A. in Communications from Concordia University, St. Paul.

Printed in the United States
By Bookmasters